THE MAN WHO SCARED

NOEL BOIVIN comes by his credentials for this book honestly. He's been known to enjoy the odd fermented beverage during his recreational hours, and his apt surname—the French translation is Drinkwine—can be found on vineyards in the Normandy region of France. His hometown of St. Catharines, Ontario, is known for its Grape and Wine Festival, which he faithfully tries to attend every year.

Boivin has divided much of his time since journalism school between freelance writing and travel, including a stint living in Shanghai. He now resides in Bangkok, Thailand, where he works for an English-language daily newspaper and as a freelancer, and from which base he continues to explore Southeast Asia.

After eking out a science degree from the University of Toronto, focusing his efforts more on reading books of the non-course-related variety, CHRISTOPHER LOMBARDO turned his attention to journalism school, from which he dropped out to pursue freelancing and write books such as this one.

He is an accomplished guitarist, and a less-than-accomplished recreational boxer, though he can claim to own a novelty "smiley face" punching pen. Lombardo speaks Italian very badly, German less so, and his loyalties are divided along these, his ethnic lines, every World Cup tournament. He makes his home in downtown Toronto.

the man who scared a shark to death and other true tales of drunken debauchery

Noel Boivin and
Christopher Lombardo

PENGUIN
CANADA

PENGUIN CANADA

Published by the Penguin Group

Penguin Group (Canada), 90 Eglinton Avenue East, Suite 700, Toronto, Ontario, Canada M4P 2Y3
   (a division of Pearson Canada Inc.)

Penguin Group (USA) Inc., 375 Hudson Street, New York, New York 10014, U.S.A.
Penguin Books Ltd, 80 Strand, London WC2R 0RL, England
Penguin Ireland, 25 St Stephen's Green, Dublin 2, Ireland (a division of Penguin Books Ltd)
Penguin Group (Australia), 250 Camberwell Road, Camberwell, Victoria 3124, Australia
   (a division of Pearson Australia Group Pty Ltd)
Penguin Books India Pvt Ltd, 11 Community Centre, Panchsheel Park, New Delhi – 110 017, India
Penguin Group (NZ), cnr Airborne and Rosedale Roads, Albany, Auckland 1310, New Zealand
   (a division of Pearson New Zealand Ltd)
Penguin Books (South Africa) (Pty) Ltd, 24 Sturdee Avenue, Rosebank, Johannesburg 2196,
   South Africa

Penguin Books Ltd, Registered Offices: 80 Strand, London WC2R 0RL, England

First published 2006

(WEB)   10 9 8 7 6 5 4 3 2 1

LIBRARY AND ARCHIVES CANADA CATALOGUING IN PUBLICATION

Boivin, Noel, 1978–

   The man who scared a shark to death : and other true tales of drunken debauchery /
Noel Boivin and Christopher Lombardo.

ISBN-13: 978-0-14-305211-1
ISBN-10: 0-14-305211-X

1. Alcoholism—Anecdotes. 2. Alcoholics—Anecdotes.
I. Lombardo, Christopher, 1974– II. Title.

HV5068.B63   2006   362.292   C2006-904914-9

Visit the Penguin Group (Canada) website at **www.penguin.ca**

Special and corporate bulk purchase rates available; please see
www.penguin.ca/corporatesales or call 1-800-399-6858, ext. 477 or 474

With thanks to my uncle Ken Boivin,
and in memory of
my grandfather Albert Boivin (1922–2006). NB

Contents

Introduction

Often people display a curious respect for a man drunk, rather like the respect of simple races for the insane. There is something awe-inspiring in one who has lost all inhibitions. Of course we make him pay afterward for his moment of superiority, his moment of impressiveness.
—F. SCOTT FITZGERALD, *TENDER IS THE NIGHT*

Getting drunk gives people free rein to behave in any reckless, ribald way conceivable, comforting themselves later with the fact that they "wouldn't have done *that* sober!" Indeed, many of us have at some point or another said to ourselves that drinking liberally on an empty stomach is perhaps unwise—only to take the gamble, order another drink and let the devil play out the details.

What usually results are stories that, for better or worse (sadly, usually the latter), we will hear recounted for the rest of our lives. Many of us may have had second thoughts about keeping the same high school friends, knowing we'll cringe upon hearing the thousandth recounting of the time Kellerman, drunk on Schnapps, scaled that big tree in front of his house, only to lose his nerve on the descent and require an early morning rescue by groggy firefighters.

The Monday morning following an office party is a fertile time for the exchange of such tales: ones about photocopied rear-ends, dancing that had to that point been reserved strictly for the bedroom mirror, the dressing down of higher-ups with a verve that only booze can bring, or an impromptu office hook-up that began under the mistletoe and ended with a silent awkward cup of coffee the next morning. Hangovers make us question, at least temporarily, why we indulge in an activity that brings enjoyment to one's life and yet culminates in such unpleasant physical symptoms—which of course grow worse when paired with the obligation to apologize for something: a professional gaffe, irreparable damage done to a personal relationship, a tattoo extolling one's admiration for dragons, wizardry and wolves by moonlight.

If you have found yourself in this position at one point or another, take heart, for you are statistically unlikely to be included in this book.

The drunken exploits chronicled in *The Man Who Scared a Shark to Death* eclipse those that occur at your average corner bar. These people have gone above and beyond the call of duty to entertain us with standard lampshade-dancing fare and caught the attention of newspapers. Scouring through broadsheets from around the world, we put together a group that represents the summit of achievement among excessive drinkers. You can gape in awe at these standout members of the boozing set for their moments of impressiveness or you can simply read these tales to take your mind off your suffering when a hangover settles in.

And the next time you get ready to unscrew that bottle of plonk fermenting in the back of Uncle Wally's shed, think back on these cautionary tales. Or better yet, don't—and give us plenty of material for a sequel.

À votre santé!
NB & CL

I

Work Is the Curse of the Drinking Class: Liquid Lunches, Study Break Benders and Lush Leisure Pursuits

According to that neighbour's houseguest who spends his afternoons swinging on a hammock and sipping rum out of a coconut, life is about finding just the right balance among work, school and play.

From an early age, however, we realize that time is often not under our control. When you're a kid, as the school year draws to a close and you'd rather be stretched out on the sofa shaking out the remains of a bag of Doritos, you're instead forcibly shunted off to a children's camp where some taskmaster forces you to construct crappy folk art out of elbow macaroni and paper plates. Authority figures such as these give you a taste of what the heavily regimented workaday world is all about—putting up with someone else's insane demands while trying to stay sane yourself.

For members of the white-collar set, the after-work cocktail is something to look forward to after sitting at a computer for hours on end, doing buttocks clenches or whatever else you can to ward off the physically deteriorating effects of such a lifestyle. If you're unfortunate enough to work in an office environment so oppressive that somebody with a stopwatch and a clipboard could conceivably scrutinize the time you've spent in the bathroom, for example, then you may very well see the appeal of eschewing solid food on your lunch hour.

University or college is where we are ostensibly sent to learn workplace-relevant skills. In actuality what these environments provide is a grounding in the best way to escape the looming drudgery of office life: excessive drinking.

Tipsy teachers are covered here, but attention is also paid to the youth of tomorrow, who the media assures us are precocious, technologically savvy video-game wizards, but who we think, judging from the sample assembled here, could be a cause for alarm.

Adding an even darker shade of grey to this particular cloud is the fact that for many people the only outlet for escaping the rigours of exam time or 80-hour workweeks is a dogged, unflinching support for bloated sports teams made up of athletes who learned all they needed to know on the playground and still managed to become millionaires. Life, as any spirit-crippling parent will tell you, is anything but fair. Sports tops even personal misfortune, bad relationships and group bitch-fests about work as the number one reason people get together to drink. Some of the more unheralded lights in the world of sports—the fans, officials and even a chess player with an overactive bladder—are given blue-ribbon recognition here.

1

Suits Gone Wild: When the Tie Is Loosened and So Are the Standards

Life is like high school with money.

—FRANK ZAPPA

Take This Job and Shove It (but Don't Fire Me or I'll Sue)

THE SCOTSMAN, MARCH 1996

A chief danger of office parties is the risk you run of getting so sloppy drunk that you actually say to your superiors the things that you had previously only dreamed about over pints with your colleagues. Provided it's a job you want to hold on to and one that is keeping a roof over your head, it is never prudent to besmirch the character of your boss or pitch insults at the firm—at least not while higher-ups are within earshot. As they say in Japan, where workplace conformity is the rule, "The nail that sticks out gets hammered back in."

The champion of our first story is a Scottish account executive who sued after the hammer of discipline pounded him.

The executive, 39, was inebriated when speaking at a sportsmen's dinner in 1994, and told the crowd how the previous Christmas, in lieu of the holiday bonus he had been expecting, he had received a packet of soiled underwear and a signed note thanking him for his accomplishments that year. (We can only hope that he was speaking in a metaphorical sense.)

He went on to tell off his current superiors in clear, unambiguous ways and, for those in the audience who were not fluent in the deciphering of the writing on the wall, he also announced that he was leaving to set up his own firm.

The executive apparently was not planning to leave the firm immediately and over the next couple of days he apologized to his superiors. A few days later, he was called in to what was purportedly a sales and business direction meeting. He arrived to find that due to his drunken and unorthodox speech, instead of examining pie charts with a laser pointer, he was being shown the door.

Fortunately for him, a tribunal ruled that the speech was merely a "drunken ramble" and did not constitute a fireable offence. They ordered the company to pay the man £6,841, less 10 percent due to the man's own bad behaviour in the situation. The exec in question, not surprisingly, left to captain a consultancy firm of his own.

How to Thrash Friends and Injure People

NCR Tribune (India), August 2002

Dale Carnegie, the grandfather of all motivational hacks, spouted the following grammatically faulty platitude: "Act enthusiastic and you will be enthusiastic." The authors prefer Fred Flintstone's catch-all: "Think big, be big, Barney." Nonetheless, those working in marketing and advertising are forced to read tomes filled with this kind of stuff, memorize it and try to "actualize it" in their daily lives, so it should come as no surprise if they do, on occasion, go berserk.

Employees at a private advertising firm in India, likely straining under the weight of Carnegie's modern-day subcontinental equivalents, turned a business dinner thrown by their firm into a drag-'em-out battle royal on the company's tab. At a high-level meeting of 100 of the firm's executives held at a hotel in New Delhi, alcohol was served and consumed in great quantities, after which the advertising folk began to run amok through the building, leaving in their wake more shattered glass and tableware than at a Greek wedding.

As the supplies of food and drink dwindled, the execs battled among themselves, throwing beer and whisky bottles at one another and pausing only to thrash any member of the hotel staff unfortunate enough to intervene.

Security guards eventually resorted to firing their revolvers into the air and cops rushed to the scene. The nine executives taken into police custody were so incorrigible at the station that they had to be doused with buckets of cold water.

The Camera Adds Ten Rounds

THE INDEPENDENT (U.K.), JUNE 2002

We are reluctant to include journalists in a chapter entitled Suits Gone Wild as their standards of personal dress are typically looser than Aunt Betty's belt at the annual all-you-can-shuck clam cook-off, but since news anchors are typically immaculately attired (at least from the desk up) we figured their addition wouldn't ruffle any ascots.

An Irish journalist's sounding off while drunk on a public television station ranks up there among great boob-tube moments with the first time Larry King hopped up behind his desk and took a call from Betsy in Beaver Point. If you are going to get totalled on the telly, you might as well go for the gusto and hit the viewing audience where it hurts, which to his credit this presenter did— expressing his hopes that the national soccer team would be trounced in the World Cup.

The commentator had sat slumped in his chair for the better part of the broadcast, visibly drunk. When he did perk up it was to chime in with abuse for the national team, saying that he hoped they would be routed by Germany and Saudi Arabia in their World Cup matches. The station said that his drunken on-air babble failed to constitute "World Cup analysis" as was required in his hefty contract. That and 1,300 angry calls from viewers beside themselves at the statements of the national icon led to his suspension.

DISHONOURABLE MENTION
The Broadsheet Bullies

There are many different ways to deal with workplace grievances. You can stuff the suggestion box with profanity-riddled anonymous messages, take 30-minute union-approved bathroom breaks, abscond with rolls of toilet paper in your backpack, or, if these measures prove fruitless, consider more extreme actions.

In Belgrade, Yugoslavia, cops had to be called in when a bunch of newspaper workers, angered by recent layoffs, did just that—getting drunk and locking the publisher in his office.

The newspaper, which was selling only a few thousand copies a day due to an ill-advised throwing of its editorial support behind "The Butcher of the Balkans," Slobodan Milosevic, had recently stopped its print run and had laid off half its staff, thus spurring the newsies' revolt.

Police managed to free the publisher of the once leading state-sanctioned peddler of government lies after just a few hours and without violence. The "stop the presses!" lever, which, if we know anything about the inner workings of the newspaper business, probably had its protective glass case smashed, was reset and the plagued scandal sheet got back to business. (Associated Press, U.S., November 2003)

Who's That Fumbling at My Door?

DAILY TELEGRAPH (AUSTRALIA), JULY 2005

After a long night of gulping back whisky-and-Cokes, throwing your back out on the mechanical bull, straining your vocal cords and breaking crystal glasses by scaling previously untouched heights on the karaoke machine, sometimes all you want to do is have a good night's sleep so you can live to drink another day.

That's all a drunken banker from Sydney wanted in July 2005 when he got home at 1:30 A.M. The 35-year-old had already been out bending his elbow all night at bars by the time he arrived completely legless at his apartment complex.

He entered his building but had difficulty opening his apartment door. This is not unusual, as anyone who has fumbled with keys while inebriated will know; however, he should have clued in that something was up when a strange woman answered.

In his befuddled state, he wasn't about to ask any questions. The banker grabbed the woman by her T-shirt, pulled her out of the apartment, staggered in and slammed the door behind him.

The woman, who had been apartment-sitting for her daughter, pounded on the door for 10 minutes to no avail before summoning police. Forcing their way into the apartment they found the naked intruder passed out face down on the bed. They roused him by dumping a glass of cold water over his head, but when they told him to get dressed, he laughed in their faces and refused.

Police said the man stank of booze and that he had passed the point of comprehension, but eventually they managed to haul him out. Once he sobered up he was contrite, and as his barrister told the judge, the banker had believed the flat to be his own and that was the only explanation he had for his bizarre actions. The sympathetic judge decided not to record a conviction against him.

2
Halls of Drunker Learning: Grade A Boozing

You have four years to be irresponsible here. Relax. Work is for people with jobs ...Go out on a Tuesday with your friends when you have a paper due Wednesday. Spend money you don't have. Drink 'til sunrise. The work never ends, but college does ..."

—TOM PETTY

Rhodes Scholar

AGENCE FRANCE-PRESSE, JULY 2002; BBC, JULY 2002;
DAILY TELEGRAPH (AUSTRALIA), JULY 2002

Whether the choice of destination is some tropical island, Spain, Mexico, the Florida Keys or, as in this case, a Greek resort, it seems to be a matter of course for university or college students to require at least one brief holiday of debauchery per year. It is here that they are able to "let their hair down" (read: indulge in boozing and illicit sex the likes of which would have sent Caligula scurrying back to his room in disgust) and escape the rigours of "academic" life.

Owing to the fact that university kids typically are not cash-rich—this owing no doubt as much to their bar tabs as educational expenses—resort areas offering package deals are usually the ones sought out for these youthful expeditions.

A British university student, age 20, caused something of an international incident on one such week-long, £320 holiday at a beach resort on the Greek island of Rhodes.

This "Rhodes Scholar" was drinking cocktails at £1 a pop with friends when a bus carrying just-arrived Britons drove past. To herald the newcomers, the student and his mates opted not to wave but rather to welcome them in another way. "In the 'time-honoured' manner of greeting, we 'mooned' them," he later said. Mooning, for the uninitiated, means showing one's bare arse in public to provoke or offend—doctor's visits don't count.

Greek police, cracking down on complaints at the resort area, caught the man's bottom-most display, singled him out and hauled him in to the local police station.

Dispensing with formality, the cops chose to refer to the man as "English scum," which, though we can't reveal his identity, was not his Christian name. Greeted thusly, he was then blindfolded, driven out to a local jail and kept in a filthy, cockroach-infested cell without food or water for 12 hours.

In what might be the harshest punishment for mooning this side of a Singaporean caning, the vacationer was told that he would face an additional 30 days in the slammer if he did not pony up €600 and sign a statement that was, literally, Greek to him.

Will This Be on the Exam?

MAINICHI NATIONAL NEWS (JAPAN), MAY 2002

For every college or university student there is that one memorable instructor—the one who inspired us *not* to come to class. You know the one: droning on from the same time-capsule–relevant notes that look like decades-old newspaper clippings kept in a shut-in's garage, or what would fall out of a hobo's pockets if you shook him upside down.

At a university in Fukuoka, Japan, students were treated to a lecture in which the marketing prof arrived late, rambled on and on about the one topic and wrote blackboard notes that were illegible (in short, duplicating every class the authors themselves recall having attended). The problem, which students brought to the attention of the administration, was that the lecturer was wasted. Clearly having missed his own lecture on the importance of professionalism and making a good impression, the academic had been swilling beer and sake during an afternoon party before his evening class.

Given the importance in the Japanese culture of saving face, the moment when officials were forced to rush into the room, stop the class and usher the drunken prof out the door, permanently, was likely extremely awkward.

The dean of the university issued an apology to those who returned to class the week following the prof's drunken swansong.

Class Trippin'

NEWSDAY (U.S.), FEBRUARY 2006

Parental release forms are a great way to eliminate a school's culpability in the event of something going horribly awry on a class trip—

little Simon getting electrocuted at that power plant visit, or Loretta wandering into the zoo's polar bear enclosure.

While parents may be consumed with worry about little Simon (having already survived the charged incident down at the plant, and now a hog-tied human pretzel crossing his skis and face-planting his way down the slopes), behaviour outside of the prescribed activity is usually not much of a concern.

On a Vermont high-school ski trip, however, it was. Depending on whom you ask, the class trip for a group of Long Island, New York, high-school students was "pretty bitchin'" (or whatever term is in the snowboarding vernacular at print time) or, according to cops, "one of the worst ski groups seen in recent history."

The students, who likely were omitted thereafter from alumni updates posted on their institution's website, smuggled bottles of booze and drugs on board the bus. The charter company Action Tours lived up to its name, as the driver had to pull over five times to settle down the increasingly bombed passengers.

A student organizer conceded later that things had gone downhill right after they left the parking lot. The driver even considered bringing an early end to the inauspicious trip—before the bus even reached the slopes. And at a fast-food restaurant in Connecticut, when one female student complained about not feeling well, it was discovered that someone had slipped something into her drink.

At the ski resort, the general manager said she received about 30 complaints from guests (or approximately one complaint for every 2.53 students, for those of you doing work at home for extra credit). The GM, who was quoted as saying that the students behaved as if they owned the place (a statement at least mildly insulting to the actual owner), called the cops in for backup.

The fuzz arrived to get a whiff of puff-the-magic-dragon and spot broken bottles in many of the rooms. By the time the trip was over, several students had been arrested for underage drinking and one had had to be hospitalized. Eighty students signed up for the trip, but only 19 ever actually took to the slopes.

If You Don't Like the Way I Drive Drunk, Stay Off the Sidewalk

DAILY TELEGRAPH (U.K.), MARCH 2004

"Those that can, do; those that can't, teach" is a common adage, especially among those whose memories of teachers consist of yardsticks across the knuckles and hands stained white from having to write out lines on the chalkboard during detention. Those that can't teach apparently take it out on their students by playing car tag (or car "it" to our U.K. friends).

Parents and concerned citizens called for the resignation of a Kent high-school teacher, whose drunken driving episode in his school's parking lot made him, they said, a "laughingstock" in the community.

The teacher had enjoyed a drunken Valentine's Day lunch with his wife before returning to school for the afternoon. Later, feeling the need for some munchies, he headed out to a Chinese takeout joint (or "takeaway" to our U.K. friends) for some grub.

Exiting his parking space, he backed over two of his students, who were atop mopeds. To make matters worse, after knocking down the pair (who, judging by the incident, would definitely get an

F for their slow reflexes), the trashed teacher took no notice of them and continued on to the restaurant.

One of the students suffered a dislocated shoulder and bruises, while the other sustained minor injuries. As for the teacher, he received a 20-month driving ban and a £300 fine—but surprisingly, to the chagrin of the parents of the parking-pylon two, the support of his headmaster and colleagues.

Did They Tell You This in History Class?

The *Mayflower*, known for bringing pilgrims to America, was more commonly used to transport booze between Spain and England. (Absolutetrivia.com)

One-Horse Town

Houston Chronicle, February 1994

Prior to advances in modern veterinary science, it was common practice (and considered humane) to put a horse with a broken leg out of its misery by shooting it. However, let it be said that there were no known medical problems ailing the two horses and a donkey that were whacked by a couple of drunken high-school seniors out on a lark in Texas.

With their parents away, the pair spent a day chugging beer, got, in their own words, "drunk and stupid," and decided to grab a rifle and hop in a pickup for an impromptu shootin' safari in Harris County.

First stop, a wide-open pasture where Junior, a donkey that had starred in church nativity scenes for years and become a community fixture, was grazing. One student jacked up the hapless burro with a rifle blast before the pair made their way farther down the road and spotted and knocked off a pair of former Olympian and rodeo-prospect horses as part of their equine extirpation.

News of the horse homicides and ass assassination shocked the community. Schoolchildren tied ribbons on the fence surrounding Junior's pasture and wept for weeks. The prosecutor received a deluge of letters from the community, many of them offering "novel approaches" to sentencing. One of the more interesting ones came from a young girl who thought the teens should be punished in the same way her dad punished her older brother for shooting black-birds: "Make them eat them."

While it is illegal to eat horsemeat in Texas, and shunned in most of the United States given the horse's near-mythological status, the French, Italians, Swiss and Japanese feel no such reluc-tance. That considered, the girl's suggestion hardly seems like much of a punishment.

Instead, the presiding judge sentenced them to a period of commu-nity service, and in addition, instructed them to attend Alcoholics Anonymous meetings three times a week, call a probation officer every day, be in their houses by midnight and not out before 5 A.M.; and forbade them from driving, drinking, using drugs or hanging out together—in effect, robbing them of the best years of their lives.

(Fund) Raising the Wrist

ROCKY MOUNTAIN NEWS (U.S.), NOVEMBER 2004

Stationary bike races for paraplegics, charity concerts for the deaf, or the sale of chocolate bars door-to-door for the diabetes association, while inappropriate, do not approach the level of fundraiser impropriety found here.

A bar in Colorado decided to hold an event to raise funds for an alcohol education program. The event was called "Wrestle-O," and according to the organizer—we kid you not—it was "the first of what were supposed to be five tournament-style gelatine-wrestling matches."

Though the report did not elaborate as to what exactly constitutes a "tournament-style gelatine-wrestling match," it turns out that part of the allure for visitors attending this spectacle was that the first 100 women in attendance received free Jell-O shots, sickly sweet concoctions of vodka-saturated frozen Jell-O.

Tackier than the gelatine wrestling itself was the fact that the education program meant to benefit from this event was established in the name of a college student who had drunk herself to death the previous September.

The deceased girl's parents issued a statement lambasting the organizers of the event for their gross insensitivity, as did the state's lieutenant governor, who called the event "irresponsible and absolutely in poor taste."

While the authors have a great respect for gelatine, and also wet lettuce-based public wrestling exhibitions, this is indeed taking things too far. The organizer was contrite following the event and the reaction it drew from the girl's parents and the public, saying that he had meant no harm and that it was just his bar's attempt "to be part of the community."

UI at DUI Class

THE ASSOCIATED PRESS, JULY 2002

It's a rite of passage, a crossroads, one of the defining moments of one's young existence, marking the transition from adolescence to adulthood. No, it's not the first encounter with a stripper, it's that pivotal point when, decked out in mortar board and gown, you shake the dean's scaly hand, whistle "Pomp and Circumstance" and step forward to claim your diploma.

But what exactly takes place at a DUI (driving under the influence) school convocation?

After 24 hours of classes, taught by caring and experienced instructors (though we're uncertain exactly *what* kind of experience they bring to the table) with a possible double minor in relapse prevention and anger management, you're once again ready to take on that world, get behind the wheel and assume your rightful, less bleary-eyed place between the yellow lines on the nation's highways.

In Iowa City, eight students did not graduate with honours from this form of continuing education. Authorities arrested eight teens taking part in a weekend-long court-ordered substance-abuse program after they were caught guzzling hooch—on "campus."

Seven of those arrested at the intensive 48-hour program were underage. The arrests were made at a class being held at a motel run by the local community college and used by the courts to treat first-time offenders. Local fuzz provide overnight security.

Police allege that one of the attendees—not the valedictorian by any means—slipped out of the motel during a break to procure some canned heat. His classmates gathered in his dorm room, sharing 1.75-litre bottles of vodka, and were caught when their boisterousness aroused suspicion.

Local police and program officials praised their capture, but conceded that efforts to closely monitor the student body were made difficult by the fact that the class was overbooked and the motel was full with regular patrons.

What are the warning signs you're staying in a fleabag motel? Well, fleas for starters. Mould, the smell of Clorox and stains on the sheets are all potential warning signs to which you can now add "High-security DUI school dorms, rooms 37 through 49."

The City That Never Sleeps It Off

A drinking establishment is now located in the New York City building that once housed the National Temperance Society. (*The Ultimate Book of Beer Trivia*, 1994)

The Aztec Two-Step Express

THE HERALD (U.K.), DECEMBER 1993

The great peril of getting sloshed while on a long-distance bus or train trip is the risk you run of being struck by the immediate need to vacate your bowels when your only option is the cramped, filthy facilities provided. Of course, as a 24-year-old student demonstrated, improvisation is always an option.

The university undergrad boarded a train from Portsmouth to London after a night of heavy drinking to celebrate his rugby club's victory, and was, as he later said, in a "drunken stupor" by the time he took his seat.

As the train was slowly moving and awaiting clearance to enter Waterloo station, Montezuma took his revenge on the stewed scrum-half. With nature sounding its most urgent call, the student, too drunk to find the train's toilet, found himself instead in the guard's station aboard the train. Unfortunately for him (but fortunately for the guard) there was nobody there to stop him from going any farther.

He opened the booth's outer door, and as he was hanging out of the train and fertilizing the passing countryside, another train rushed toward his in the opposite direction. It tore off the open door to the guard's compartment and very nearly missed making that drunken movement his last.

A guard arrived too late and could do nothing more than stand gape-mouthed at the sight of the student dangling out of his compartment. The undergrad was arrested at Waterloo and later made to pay a fine to reimburse the train for damages.

Wasted Youth

Townsville Bulletin (Australia), January 2006

Short of sending their wayward teens to juvenile boot camp, military reform school or other criminal apprenticeship programs, there is seemingly little parents can do. The threat "This is going on your permanent record, young man" doesn't seem to have the clout it once did, accompanied as it was by that old cane across the buttocks. This was made strikingly clear by a group of West Australian teens.

Sixty raging, wasted youth descended on a suburban area, smashing beer bottles, scattering mail everywhere and, what with the heavy beer consumption, getting on people's nerves with their pressing need to urinate. One drunken participant asked a resident if he could use her toilet, while another less outwardly sociable boy literally took matters into his own hands and urinated on a fence.

The congregation of drunken teens appeared to be without a purpose, as one resident said they were roaming the streets with no loud music or other signs of a party anywhere in the area.

Even without a soundtrack, the hooligans took their toll on the residential neighbourhood. "They stole my toys … they destroyed my brother's helmet," chirped a child following the incident. Silver lining, though: his brother's head was not in said helmet at the time.

A cop car and paddy wagon were dispatched to the scene to round up the teens, and the actions of that group of sixty led to police being given sweeping new "move-on" powers to deal with such roaming bands of teenage ne'er-do-wells.

To the Manor Bombed

DAILY TELEGRAPH (U.K.), SEPTEMBER 2005; *THE GUARDIAN* (U.K.), SEPTEMBER 2005

England's Marlborough College claims many distinguished past pupils, including John Hunt, leader of the first successful ascent of Mount Everest, and the great English actor James Mason, of *Julius Caesar* and *Lolita* fame. Considerably less noteworthy are Chris de Burgh, who penned "Lady in Red," a song known to clear a dance floor faster than an inopportune bout of flatulence, and Kate Middleton, the girlfriend of Prince William, known for, well, being the girlfriend of Prince William.

Less noteworthy still is a 13-year-old, to-the-manor-born and too-young-to-be-named-here scion, who was told not to return to the £22,000-per-term college because of his disciplinary record. School officials claimed it was one of the absolute worst they could recall. The young squire had spit the silver spoon out of his mouth and decided in its absence to insert a bottle and swig with abandon. A police constable found him sprawled out on a park bench with a "pile of spittle" at his side along with a couple of bottles of wine.

The boy, who was obviously not in a position to ask the bobby to take him on a ride-along, shouted: "Police are all f—ing scum," and accused the officer of assault when he handcuffed him, adding, "You're in so much f—ing trouble."

The incident got the boy booted from the prestigious school, a move that caused his father, a millionaire real-estate maven, to take up a civil action, which he later lost. He later said that he had no desire for the fruit of his loins to be reinstated, witness statements made available to the press having shamed him and the college in equal measure.

According to the school's headmaster, the father was of the school of parenting that maintains that when a problem arises with your child it is best to grab cash with both hands, take aim and throw. In keeping with this strategy, the boy's father had offered to pay a student sharing a dorm room with the apple of his eye £500 if his son's grades improved.

Moreover, and equally crippling his son's chances of becoming someone that anybody would like in his later years, the father showed no signs of embarrassment at his boy's actions, according to the headmaster, and was always antagonistic when called to discuss his escapades.

Piss-Tank Prodigy

THE SUN (U.K.), MARCH 2006

Every field of endeavour seems to have its share of precocious young savants as skilled or more so than their older counterparts; whether it's a 10-year-old who can fly a plane or Bobby Fischer before he went to Japan and became insane. The field of drunk driving is no exception.

A Berkshire teenage girl with a rap sheet already longer than the soup kitchen lineup in Bum Town was back in court to face drunk driving charges—this her second court appearance on such charges after having been forbidden from getting behind the wheel at the age of 12.

At 14, Britain's youngest ever drunk driver was sporting a gleaming, all-white Ali G–inspired tracksuit and gold chain ensemble that blinded the eyes of those assembled in the courtroom. The belligerent teen, when sentenced to a stint in the joint, got a meagre measure of revenge by kicking over a chair, leaping forward and clocking the Crown prosecutor. As the remaining powdered wigs beat a hasty retreat, she hurled a jug of water in their direction, culminating in the halting of the trial proceedings.

Before the donnybrook, the magistrate had taken the unusual step of allowing the underage offensive offender to be named, ruling that the public interest in the case outweighed the court's duty to protect her privacy—but we, being fearful of the little monster, have not made the same call.

The court heard that the girl's most recent joyriding jag at 14 was similar to a stunt she pulled on Christmas Day when she was 12 and decided to get behind the wheel of her papa's car after downing several cans of lager.

Upon her arrest, the foul-mouthed lass cursed a Legion Hall–worthy blue streak at police: "What the f—k are you doing here! For f—k's sake."

The girl, flanked by her family, penitently explained to the bench how she had mended her ways, a claim undermined somewhat by her arrival at court earlier that day to launch eggs at the press gallery.

3
Unsportsmanlike Conduct and Other Assorted Drinking Games

Sports serve society by providing vivid examples of excellence.

—GEORGE F. WILL

The Fall of the Roamin' Umpires

JERUSALEM POST, SEPTEMBER 1999

Being a soccer referee entails having to duck Gatorade-infused expectorant from offending players, wearing ill-fitting short pants and often being held personally responsible for fatal stompings, fired-off flares or full-blown riots in the stands.

Apparently, the rigours of being athletic adjudicators were too much for four Russian match officials to bear, causing them to snap and go completely gonzo shortly before taking charge of a UEFA European Cup game between an Israeli and a Belgian club.

The raucous Russian refs landed drunk at Ben Gurion Airport, and upon exiting the aircraft broke out into an off-the-cuff song-and-dance routine. Rather than receiving applause or having a hat passed around for their efforts, they were met by airport police, women in this case—whom they then proceeded to fondle.

The local escort assigned to the unctuous umps spoke to police on their behalf to prevent their incarceration and whisked them off to a Tel Aviv bistro. Here, before you could slur *"Na zdorovje,"* the officials were back at it, kissing the hands of waitresses, pinching them and insisting that their glasses be filled with whisky. To prevent his staff from being further mauled by the randy referees, the owner of the bistro eventually had to swap his waitresses for waiters.

With nary a hand to kiss nor a woman to molest, the soccer refs decided to take their show outdoors. Striding out to the middle of the road sans whistle, the foursome began directing street traffic.

Afterwards, the frivolous four faced serious sanctions for their actions, while emergency replacement officials had to be rushed from Bucharest to attend to the match that they had been set to call.

The True Legend of the Drunken Chess Master, or Pissing Off the Bishop

TORONTO STAR, MARCH 2005

Babe Ruth is said to have enjoyed running up and down train aisles completely blotto and punching out the straw hats of his fellow passengers when his team was on the road. Since those halcyon days, which like other halcyon days were designated as such dozens of years later by people who weren't actually there to remember them, the image of the merry sportsman has become a recognizable figure.

While some may argue that chess is not a sport, because you could theoretically play the game using only your tongue, we beg to differ and point to the Olympic committee's decision to include it among their events. And just like baseball and football, chess too has its stories of athletes taking to the drink and unleashing the results on an unsuspecting public.

An international chess master cemented his reputation at a tournament match where he launched a move heretofore unheard of among the game's generals. Dubbed by chess wags the "Open Fly Gambit," it entails breaking play to open one's pants and shooting a stream of piss at the board.

Round three of the showdown coincided with the chess master's birthday, and rather than sacrificing the special day for chess, a monotonous game he probably plays every day of the year, he chose to go to a bar and get sloppy drunk. He arrived at the game in a dozy beer funk, laid his head down on the table and went to sleep, only to be jolted awake by his ringing cell phone.

Upon awakening, the copious amounts of beer he had drunk were pushing him for an immediate exit and, according to a chess association report, "He stood up, unzipped his pants, pulled out his manhood, and urinated all over the table, the chess pieces, and board and on the floor."

The Open Fly Gambit has yet to be repeated at international chess matches.

Pee Pee Le Feu

DAILY TELEGRAPH (AUSTRALIA), JULY 1998; CNN, JULY 1998

The Tomb of the Unknown Soldier from the Second World War was interred beneath Paris's Arc de Triomphe on Armistice Day in 1920 and an "eternal flame" was also lit there to honour France's war dead.

There are numerous eternal flames around the world meant to symbolize how the memory of someone or something will never fade from the collective consciousness—and they are not to be confused with the saccharine pop-tune "Eternal Flame," which hopefully will.

The flame was the first of its kind in Western Europe, and aside from an incident in 1997 in which an Australian was arrested for trying to cook an egg over it, it burned on and on without incident—until 1998, that is, when the World Cup came to town.

Visitors from around the globe poured in to witness the spectacle of the World Cup in the country where the idea for the event is thought to have originated. The French enjoyed hosting the event and ultimately the result—France rousted Brazil in the final—but, one incident put a bit of a, tut-tut, damper on the proceedings.

Two drunken World Cup fans visiting from Mexico proved that eternity is too lofty a goal to shoot for and doused the Arc de Triomphe's "eternal" flame by urinating on it. Relaying this news to the French public, the country's defence ministry said that the flame was "soiled" in an "unspeakable act."

The pair responsible, a man and a woman, were arrested on charges of "offending the dead" as well as being drunk in public; however, they were later released without convictions being recorded.

Mead Stampede

Australian Associated Press, October 1987

Nothing brings out the best in people like a rodeo. Rodeo clowns, not there for a laugh or to give you nightmares like normal clowns, make sure Man Versus Bull is a fair fight by evening out the 3,800-pound weight differential, an integral part of the goings-on, lest the off-his-gourd cowboy is, well, gored.

The events, though, often draw clowns of another sort, who, while sporting red noses, can't be counted on to do amusing tricks with balloons.

In Western Australia, in a burg more far flung than a beer bottle in a police riot, the annual rodeo can be counted on to swell the ranks of the town's population from 700 to 2,000, as well as its jail space. Like hotel beds at Mardi Gras, drunk-tank accommodation at the rodeo is hard to come by, and once the '87 show was underway, cops had their hands full with nearly 200 drunk-tank arrests.

The previous year, and this was quite possibly a point of distinction brought up in city council meetings, the most drunks that had spent the night in the tank was 127—a number that in '87, according to a local sergeant, they "beat well and truly."

The remote settlement, with a reputation of being Australia's roughest—in terms of that universal corporeal measure "fewest teeth per capita"—draws truckloads of people (and to this may we add that "truckloads of people" never has a positive connotation) to the three-day affair.

The beleaguered town, whose population balloons with drunk and violent revellers who "stay with relatives or simply sleep in the bush," has to deal with what cops describe as an "orgy" (and not the good kind either, with togas and grapes) until authorities are called to step in. As one officer noted: "You just bring in one load and then go out and get another."

The undersized jail has only two blocks, each with four cells, each cell designed to hold 12 inmates. In an effort to be hospitable, cops spread mattresses on the floor, but many of them slam-basted cowboys just sleep it off on the hard concrete.

In Gaol Oh? (and Other "Hooligan" Anagrams)

BBC NEWS TIMES ONLINE (U.K.), FEBRUARY 2005

Along with the traditional rites of passage into adulthood such as the bar mitzvah, convocation and voting for the first time, there are other more subjective yardsticks to determine whether a person has really put away childish things and become a grown-up. Even if your years proclaim it, you cannot take your place among other adults until you stop such behaviour as eating peas out of a tin and doing your dishes in the bathtub, and start wearing shirts that actually button up and jeans that are not mended using clothespins and masking tape.

Unfortunately there are some for whom this threshold is never crossed (and for whom there is no chromosomal deficit to explain it away), the perpetually atavistic who take great delight in activities that would embarrass a precocious 8-year-old. Add one such 42-year-old to the aforementioned.

Decades beyond being able to chalk up abject stupidity to young-at-heart exuberance, a U.K. football hooligan who already had been banned, for drunken behaviour, for three years from every stadium in England and Wales for 24 sport-related convictions gave yet another clear demonstration as to why.

During a Football Association Challenge Cup tilt, he ran out onto the pitch well into his pints, assaulted two cops and challenged a player to a fight.

A 34-year-old accomplice, meanwhile, doomed to hit the same on-ramp to the idiot highway as his fatuous friend, turned spectator activity away from the on-pitch action by reliving the 1980s: break dancing in the nude.

The man who stormed the pitch and started the brawl, already familiar with the ins and outs of the judicial system as a result of having been jailed a month for his role in another match melee, was given a five-month jail term and yet another banning order, this time of 10 years. The authors look forward to revisiting this case once that period has elapsed.

Completely Bowled Over

Sunday Herald Sun (Australia), February 2003

The sheer length of a cricket match, with its innumerable breaks for lunch, tea and scones, makes the average chess contest look like the Kentucky Derby.

Astoundingly, this genteel affair can end in a draw, even after numerous hours or even several days of play, at which point all that white cotton is taken en masse to a dry cleaner. When the game goes into its equivalent of extra innings, prepare to pack a lunch and a spare set of knickers. Given the lengthy play time, it follows that one must, on occasion, make one's own entertainment.

A high-ranking South African cricket official issued a public apology for the drunken larking about of his country's United Board president at a World Cup match.

In a tilt, the annihilated ambassador could barely stand up and had lurched from seat to private box seat, heavily favouring red wine and hurling profanities, like so many balls at a wicket, at guests.

When confronted about whether he kissed his mother with that mouth, he allegedly retorted that if he curses it is "for a good reason."

At one point during the match he wrapped his hands around the neck of a fellow spectator and is quoted as proclaiming, perhaps redundantly: "Sonny, I am so f—ing drunk I don't know where the f— I am."

The official later issued an unconditional apology, saying that his conduct was unacceptable for a man in his position—though arguably, for a man in any position.

Give me a D–R–U–N–K! What's That Spell?

THE INDEPENDENT (U.K.), SEPTEMBER 2005; BBC, OCTOBER 2005;
THE STATE (U.S.), MARCH 2006; *SAN DIEGO UNION,* NOVEMBER 2005;
NEWS 14 CAROLINA, MARCH 2006

Professional cheerleaders have to sign a contract banning them from conduct potentially embarrassing to their club. Though a detractor would say drawstring stretch pants, glittery crop tops, giant teased hair and the shouting of inane slogans constitute exactly such behaviours, these are not proscribed in law.

Two former cheerleaders were toasting their team's fortune in a bar when they ignored the needs of fellow patrons by hogging a bathroom stall together. Exactly *what* the pair was up to in there is a matter of conjecture, with some witnesses claiming to have overheard their amorous exploits. Truth be told, this was a charge they would later deny—but don't let that stop your imagination from running wild.

What we do know is that when the door opened and the pair was confronted by an angry woman whose bladder was about to explode, one of the pompom perps popped her in the face. Her friend, no less a hothead, was later brought up on charges of disorderly conduct and resisting arrest. The iron-fisted cheerleader promptly made matters worse by offering up to authorities a phoney driver's licence.

The K.O. Queen, who now has a tale to recount to future grandkids about what a halter-top-wearing firebrand Granny used to be, was ordered to pay $400 in restitution for rearranging the face of the weak-bladdered plaintiff.

Her partner in crime was charged with 50 hours of community service, which may or may not have included mowing lawns in skimpy attire.

II

Plowed Pillars of Society

In some parts of the world, having a beer in a public park or anywhere outside of a licensed establishment or a private home is a chargeable offence. This is why hobos choose to conceal their bottles of whisky and/or plonk in paper bags. Likewise, driving with an open container of booze in your car is also widely prohibited—even if you are not drinking it or, say, only taking paced-out sips to help calm your nerves in heavy traffic.

The implications of this worrying trend are frightening. Such a draconian blanket could conceivably extend to innocent people getting criminal records for any number of drinking-related violations: looking or smelling drunk could be a chargeable offence, as could shuffling to the rhythms of Latin America, playing darts poorly, hogging the Foosball table and singing off-key or along with the radio or both. Maximum penalties could arise if a panel of your closest peers disagrees with your choice of bed companions after a long night of boozing.

Fortunately, for those of us who have progressed beyond the ways of the puritan, there are still those in positions of power who, if they were to enforce such rules, could be pointed to as utter and complete hypocrites. In Plowed Pillars of Society, we are telling their stories.

Conveniently, for the authors of this book, and unfortunately for those they serve, these stories were extremely easy to find.

Licentious lawmakers are embarrassing their constituents around the world with their drunken horseplay and the public trust placed in cops, soldiers, the judiciary and medical professionals is also being strained by wild drunken antics that would put a blush on the cheeks of their supposed opposites in Crime Doesn't Pay (Your Bar Tab).

These powers-that-be-very-very-drunk give us all cause to smile when we get hassled by cops on a night out, hear a politician expounding platitudes, or, if we are truly unfortunate, are forced to listen to a lecture from a doctor or a judge. Despite their air of superiority, among their ranks and sitting in positions of equal stature alongside them are those whose stories are included here.

4

The Draft Constitution: Politicos with a Taste for the Tipple

A statesman is an easy man, he tells his lies by rote. A journalist invents his lies, and rams them down your throat. So stay at home and drink your beer and let the neighbours vote.

—WILLIAM BUTLER YEATS

Miscarriage of Justice

AGENCE FRANCE-PRESSE, SEPTEMBER 2004;
THE LOCAL (SWEDEN), SEPTEMBER 2004

Politics is fraught with stresses the likes of which most of us cannot even imagine. In fact, these stresses are *so* unimaginable that the authors could not think of a single example to give you in this regard. However, taking it for granted that the job of holding sway over the lives of your inferiors is quite stressful, it stands to reason that doing so in Sweden would also be quite taxing, though presumably to a far lesser degree.

The alcohol spokesman for the Moderate Party in Sweden was ideally suited for his portfolio. He displayed the relish with which he pursued the duties of his office by taking his young toddler along with him to attend a local wine festival in the early afternoon. The spokesman sampled the products of local vineyards not to the point of drunkenness, which would have been most immoderate for a member of his Moderate Party, but to the point at which, as he later told police in the drunk-tank, "life seemed fantastic."

Feeling acceptably "fantastic," he left the wine tasting, with his son in a pram, and shortly thereafter was spotted by a female security guard at a nearby shop running down the street with the pram. Concerned because he was staggering as he ran and on several occasions both he and the pram were nearly knocked ass over teakettle, the security guard tried to stop him. The guard alleges that the Swede then went into a frenzy and knocked her over the head.

The spokesman later apologized for the drunken pram-run, claiming that, in an apparent paranoid delusion hastened by vino, he had thought he was being chased.

He said he was embarrassed by the incident. Indeed the Swedish press, in an example of superior conjecture that we feel should be more common in reporting circles, said: "He was beyond contrite—although a stinking hangover may have had something to do with it."

A Smashing Good Bottle of Wine

Thomas Jefferson, noted, among myriad other more salacious accomplishments, for being the third president of the United States, was also an oenophile. Bottles that belonged to him, though they turned to vinegar long ago, have fetched grand sums in the past. In 1989 a New York wine owner had in his possession a bottle of Chateau Margaux 1787, on consignment from its English owner, that he was trying to unload for $500,000—a ridiculous price, which had he found a taker would have made it the most expensive bottle ever sold. He took the bottle with him to dinner at the Four Seasons, and as luck would have it a busboy bumped into his table and sent the bottle smashing to the ground. Silver lining: he had had the bottle insured for $225,000, which he then shared with its owner. (Forbes Online, December 2003)

Dipsomaniac Diplomat

PacNews (Fiji), October 2005

In preparation for the influx of randy football fans for the World Cup 2006, Berlin officials distributed 100,000 free condoms as well as leaflets on the etiquette to be observed when one frequents a prostitute. While a working version of this document was unavailable for our perusal at the time of writing, one can imagine that such a leaflet contains issues related to hygiene, safety and decorum, as well as nifty little tidbits on how to deftly bow and spin on your heel once services are rendered and money is exchanged.

Unfortunately, such codes of conduct were completely thrown out the window recently, by a Papua New Guinean diplomat no less.

The unidentified diplomat, whose offence was such that for reasons of national security and international shaming even the name of the country in which he committed the offence was left out of media reports, was the recipient of a stern rebuke from Papua New Guinea's foreign affairs and immigration minister. He warned that the PNG government would not tolerate public transgressions by members of its diplomatic service.

Reports in PNG claimed that the senior diplomat had been recalled from his post after being found asleep and drunk in a mission vehicle in front of a hotel without a shirt on and with irate prostitutes demanding payment for services rendered.

Soliciting the services of a prostitute is indeed low-level diplomacy (slightly above that of refereeing a girls' field hockey game), the mastery of which it seems would be a prerequisite for pursuing international relations, negotiating alliances, et cetera. As Henry David Thoreau once noted (perhaps not specifically referring to the soliciting of sexual favours), "That man is the richest whose pleasures are the cheapest."

Regardless, the foreign affairs minister was not pleased, and given some of the alcohol-induced shenanigans got up to by other officials of PNG (see parts of the remainder of this chapter), he had some cause to be miffed.

When MPs Attack

Herald Sun, December 2003; *The Age* (Australia), December 2003; Wikipedia.com

The decision to run for public office comes with the knowledge that whatever skeletons you have in your closet will be taken out and given a more thorough shaking than a can of paint at your local hardware store. Transgressions that go unnoticed in the life of your everyday person—greasing the palms of city inspectors so that they turn a blind eye to the flagrant violations in the slum building you operate, for example—are the sorts of stories that make journalists salivate, stroke their wispy beards and cackle fiendishly while cleaning the heads of their tape recorders with a Q-tip.

Embarrassing yourself once you're already in public office, however, is on an entirely different level, bringing into question as it does what the people who elected you were thinking when they did so.

In Australia, a member of Parliament resigned his leadership of the Democrat Party due to just such an incident, which began at a coalition Christmas barbecue held at Government House for the Democrat and Liberal parties.

The MP showed up at some point during the soiree and partook of the drinking. He was an unexpected guest at the function, but no eyebrows were raised until he tried to make off with five bottles of wine from the barbecue's supply. Taking objection to the attempted heist, Liberal staff went to retrieve the wine, returning with only four out of the five bottles.

A Liberal senator decided to take the matter up on the floor of the Senate chamber, and got more than she expected when the man, a former professional rugby player and not surprisingly a physically imposing character, shook her by the shoulder and called her a "f—ing bitch" while the rest of the Senate looked on agape.

The senator did not sustain any injuries and was willing to let the entire incident go—until, that is, the MP made an attempt at an apology: sending a card wishing her "a relaxing break" accompanied by a single bottle of wine. She responded by suggesting that he check himself in to an alcohol treatment program.

While initially stepping down due to the incident, the MP went on to retake his position as leader of the Democrats, pledging that he would swear off booze for the rest of his life. So far he seems to have stuck to that pledge, at least at public functions.

The Mayor May Not

Plain Dealer (U.S.), April 2005

A style of office, or honorific, is a form of address that by tradition or law is used for a person who holds a title or post, such as "Excellency" for archbishops and governors general and "hey, you" for the guy working behind the counter at the service station. "Your Worship" is the proper form of address for mayors, though this formality seems less than fitting for the elected official in the following story.

Acting on an anonymous phone tip about a car swerving more noticeably than Uncle Mort at a Lodge pig roast, cops finally found the mayor befuddled in a city-owned vehicle. They stopped him before he could do himself any harm, the likelihood of which was certain given that he was at the time temporarily parked outside a fast-food establishment of intestine-clogging notoriety.

The mayor, while sickening cops with his burger-and-booze-soaked exhalations, failed several sobriety tests; however, he refused to submit to a Breathalyzer.

His Worship did eventually plead no contest to the charges related to the incident and also read a prepared statement at a City Council meeting expressing his shame for the incident.

The mayor, who ironically doubles as the safety director of his village, lost his driving privileges for a year, except as required for work, an odd ruling given that the incident occurred in a vehicle running on taxpayers' gas, and after a booze-up with a female city councillor.

A Rough Day for the Dark Knight

THE GUARDIAN (U.K.), JULY 1993

Batman, as anybody whose life has been warped by inhabiting the fantasy life of comic-book superheroes will tell you, is, along with being one of the world's greatest detectives, scientists and gadgeteers, also well trained in martial arts and acrobatics.

In 1993, the Batman movie franchise was still in the hands of Tim Burton, and those T-shirts you still see on some people featuring the caped crusader's logo were actually new and just as popular as the ones with Bart Simpson telling you to "Eat My Shorts." A Labour front-bench spokesman was presumably caught up in all the dark-knight hysteria sweeping the world in the early '90s when he attempted an ill-advised stunt following a drinking bout at a reception held by a liquor association. Returning to the Commons, the MP decided to descend the steps by leaping down them "in the manner of Batman," according to *Guardian* reports, but it wasn't the Boy Wonder there to greet him upon landing.

The blasted 51-year-old apparently had not sounded the "Look out below!"—or if he did, someone didn't have her hearing aid in, because on making contact with the bottom of the stairs he also bowled over an old lady. The sozzled spokesman then tried to help the woman up, but tripped as he did so.

The woman who had intercepted this leaping-lush MP was treated for cuts and bruises and released from hospital. A government aide reported that the caped crusader was told to keep away from the Commons to avoid creating a "diversion" during Question Period.

This One's on the House

COURIER-MAIL (AUSTRALIA), MAY 1986

If we may draw an analogy, like so many cold pints from a keg, the House Speaker who presides over debates in legislative assemblies is much like your barkeep. They are responsible for maintaining order during debates, over social policy, or over whether *Gilligan's Island* was really a Marxist social critique—or, more typically, over whether the _____ [insert name of perpetually failing sports team here] can really "go all the way this year." They may and often do discipline parties who break the House/bar rules.

To further extend this analogy, which is more stretched than your boxers' waistband after Thanksgiving, both the House Speaker and the barkeep are capable of adding legitimacy to the debate, breaking the tie by casting their vote and settling barroom arguments.

In Papua New Guinea, the House Speaker's soused conduct was questioned after various witnesses reported seeing him urinate on the carpet of the parliamentary bar and added that some of his guests had also raised a ruckus at the bar. After initially denying the claims, in true political fashion he admitted that his recollections were foggy because he had been knocking 'em back.

He said that as a Seventh Day Adventist he normally abstained from the tipple. According to the group's mission statement, they advocate preaching, teaching and healing, but nowhere in the fine print does it mention anything about getting wrecked in public. Like a good Adventist, he went on to apologize to all concerned.

At the Taxipayers' Expense

COURIER-MAIL (AUSTRALIA), FEBRUARY 1989;
TORONTO STAR, FEBRUARY 1989; WIKIPEDIA.COM

Holding public office has its perks. After a life spent wildly throwing money around that was not your own to begin with, you're then rewarded with a big fat pension that is the envy of all those poor slobs who voted you in.

In Australia a Labour MP, in a brazen act of both suckling on the public teat and sucking down libations, billed taxpayers for a sizable taxi fare one night when he was too blotto to remember his own address.

After getting as pissed as a newt at the governor general's farewell feast, the MP went on a two-hour fact-finding mission through the streets of the city in search of his homestead. The cabbie, after contacting his dispatch, was advised to drive the MP wherever he wanted to go, presumably even if the request made no sense whatsoever—like when, for no apparent reason, the sloshed man asked to be taken to the airport at 2:30 A.M.

The MP eventually passed out, so the driver took him to his dispatch to look up the address in a phone book. Unfortunately, the government official had not sobered up enough to know just which of the block of units was his. Finally, after requesting a ride to another city 186 miles away, he was dropped instead at a local police station.

At the request of local cops, the MP was deposited at the parliament house with security guards there to sober up. An Administrative Services Department spokesman later defended the MP, saying that politicians were entitled to use a variety of transport, including taxis.

The Martial Arts of Diplomacy

THE ADVERTISER (AUSTRALIA), MAY 1987

For diplomats to be effective international representatives they must be skilled in clear-headed international negotiations such as those you entered into that time you talked down that shoeless market vendor for that "Antigua or bust" T-shirt on your last vacation. During one drunken evening, a Papua New Guinean diplomat in Australia employed conflict-resolution tactics that would be more suited to the Hacksaw Jim Duggan hammerlock school of negotiation.

Following a formal event, the diplomat from PNG (a country which, pound for pound, is more than amply represented in this book), his wife and an Australian diplomat went out for a dinner that they washed back with a good deal of booze. The drinks continued to flow back at the PNG diplomat's house before the trio finally decided to call it a night, and the PNG diplomat and his wife drove the Australian home, worries of a drunk-driving rap presumably quelled by the power of diplomatic privilege.

The diplomat's pie-eyed driving did not, however, escape the attention of his wife, who told him once they arrived at the Australian official's home that he was too soused to drive back to their residence. In grand drunken though not very diplomatic style, the diplomat rejected his wife's assertion and the two became embroiled in a heated disagreement.

The argument turned violent, forcing the Australian official to attempt to intervene. The PNG diplomat struck him, his wife tried to separate them and before you know it an all-out diplomatic donnybrook had broken loose in the living room as the three of them fought and bashed around the Australian's house.

The Australian got the business end of the beating, requiring an ambulance ride to the hospital where he received 11 stitches in his face due to the PNG official's blows. His house took a pounding as well. The rampaging diplomat destroyed furniture in two rooms as well as *objets d'art* in the Australian's front garden. And, in an impressive show of strength, he also broke off the Aussie's front door.

Despite the uglying his face took and the damage done to his home, the Australian chose not to press charges against his PNG counterpart owing to the long friendship the two previously enjoyed.

5

The Long Arm of the Law—
Bent at the Elbow

I'm not against the police; I'm just afraid of them.

—ALFRED HITCHCOCK

Force of Habit

COURIER-MAIL (AUSTRALIA), NOVEMBER 1987

In the late 1980s, the Fantasy Photography Studio in Australia was in full swing, and while you certainly could have had your picture taken there, that sort of thing would be secondary—and possibly blackmail-worthy—as the aptly named studio was in fact a bordello. Though photography may not have been on the top of the list of offerings at the studio, "fantasies" definitely were, and the ladies of the night working there catered to those of their clientele.

One such fantasy was the "runaway nun," played at the time by a woman with the very biblical name of Rachel. She was a particular favourite of a member of the police licensing branch, according to a woman who worked at the studio in a secretarial capacity and as a "provider of hand-relief" named "Miss Mary Brown."

The police licensing branch is responsible for ensuring that establishments selling liquor have a licence to do so, or, as in the case of the Fantasy Studio, getting freebie drinks and more at those that do not. The girls had been instructed by management to be "nice to the licensing guys," and thus the randy inspector and his licensing comrades became fixtures at the place, showing up there whether off duty or on and getting so comfortable that they began helping themselves to beer from the fridge.

During one of the inspector's visits, in a scene that could have been scripted by the late great Benny Hill, he chased Rachel the runaway nun around the brothel—"trying to lift the back of her robe," according to Miss Mary.

Of course this sort of activity was exceedingly corrupt and, like all good things, it had to come to an end. When the scandal broke, numerous embarrassing tales emerged concerning the group's drunken exploits at the studio.

Aside from the inspector's drunken nun-chasing, Miss Mary Brown told reporters, there was an occasion when the group held a "seafood banquet" at the house of ill repute to honour a colleague who, in a nice ironic twist, had just been transferred to the internal investigations department. The boys from licensing got so hammered that night that they began jumping up and down on the cathouse's mattresses, using them as trampolines.

When the Training Wheels Come Off

Associated Press, May 1989

Static training sessions are out. No longer are the participants merely torpid information receptacles, lectured to by khaki-clad clipboard-toters armed with pie charts, laser pointers and a box of day-old doughnuts. Today's training seminars employ presentation methods that are full of phoney energy, enthusiasm and a high degree of coercive participation so that workplace skills can be transferred more effectively.

Such methods were still in their testing phase back in the late '80s in small-town Indiana when a police training session was held to educate 15 volunteer reserve officers about the effects of alcohol consumption.

This particular in-house, team-building exercise in inductive inquiry involved five officers pounding back two cases of beer, two bottles of wine and a bottle of Seagram's whisky, while reserve officers, in the best Baconian tradition of scientific examination, occasionally tested them with a Breathalyzer.

In its basic form, the technique of distillation goes back thousands of years to Babylonian times, and since then, amateur experimenters (as well as your 10-year-old nephew) have perceived a strong positive correlation between alcohol intake and intoxication. This was borne out in the Indiana study as well, which was halted prematurely when a dispatch officer passed out from slugging back too much grog and had to be hauled off to a local hospital emergency room for treatment.

Stomach-pumping rookie officers was evidently not the intended outcome of the exercise, according to the town's mayor. He admitted that something had gone wrong: the drinking was supposed to have been controlled and should not have resulted in officers "getting sloppy fall-down drunk."

The police chief agreed that the methodology in this particular experiment could have stood the factoring out of at least one case of beer, and said that he was "not sure" if they would hold a similar training session again.

Ale to the Chief

San Francisco Chronicle, December 1989

There's nothing like guzzling sangria on a patio, a breeze blowing through your tousled mane, and cackling uproariously at your own slurred quips, blithely oblivious to your surroundings. In wintry climes when the temperature drops, however, you may find that you and your *bon mots* are left outside to freeze.

Of course, in more habitable environments such as sunny California, you can bring this drinking culture to the homestead, reclining in your very own patio deck chair, stirring your morning pineapple-juice-based libation with one of those little umbrellas and flipping through the funny pages in an ambrosia-infused glow, thus enjoying the very pinnacle of Left Coast living.

As a condominium owner in California found out, however, the unexpected can put a blight on your enjoyment of such sunny pleasures.

The blight in this case was none other than the city chief of police, who drunkenly lost control of his squad car, causing it to shoot off a freeway, down a 20-foot embankment, and bulldoze the condo's patio. The chief, who issued a public apology, was placed on administrative leave pending an investigation. He said that he has "always recognized the risks and dangers associated with driving while under the influence," which it seems he had now experienced first hand.

He told authorities that he swerved to avoid a car early in the A.M. that was "trying to get into his lane," perhaps referring to the imaginary "drunk driving lanes" fashioned to ease congestion and gridlock by allowing soused drivers to rear-end one another with impunity.

The chief's unmarked Ford cruiser went through the median, crossing the westbound lanes, and hurtled down the embankment, violating the rules of the big screen by not exploding immediately upon impact. It then careened through two fences before ending up on the patio.

The chief's apology "took a lot of courage," noted a city manager, but perhaps not nearly as much as does piloting your chariot down a hillside at full speed.

Seeing Double Agents: Blowing Chunks and Your Cover

ROCKY MOUNTAIN NEWS (U.S.), MAY 1994

The basic agent training curriculum for the Drug Enforcement Agency, according to its website, is a "16-week resident program that places strong emphasis upon leadership, ethics, and human dignity." Perhaps the cloak-and-dagger men in the following story excelled in other, less-qualitative aspects of the program.

A bar owner in Colorado served five graduates of this program whose drunken mania during a liquid lunch probably left him desiring a more civilized clientele—like the crack dealers these guys normally try to bust. The agents in question rang up a tab of $138—only $24 of which was spent on non-beer-and-liquor-related nutriments.

At first the bar owner said he didn't mind the rowdy behaviour of the muddled moles, saying they were "letting off steam."

But then a waitress complained that one of the agents was letting off more steam than a stink bomb in a sauna, and when she refused to pour him any more potables, the men told the bar owner that they were accustomed to drinking anytime, anywhere, and if he wasn't compliant they could shut him down. They went on to trash the bar and to let off rounds of animate throat missiles (read: vomit) as well as even scarier projectiles—rounds of live ammunition.

When the bar owner asked one of the agents to show him identification, the officer offered to produce it and shove it into the bar owner's forehead "so hard I would never forget who he was," said the unfortunate licensee.

When a deputy contacted by the proprietor later stopped a Ford Bronco in the area, two Colorado DEA agents were at the helm. Another car then pulled up driven by a DEA supervisor who had been at the tavern. He told deputies that agents had stopped for lunch and that one agent got drunk and out of control due to "recent family problems."

Although one driver's eyes were bloodshot and deputies detected a whiff of alcohol, deputies were for some mysterious reason unable to find probable cause to issue a roadside sobriety test.

Completely Absorbent

EDMONTON JOURNAL, MARCH 1999

Prometheus stole fire from mighty Zeus and gave it to primitive mortals on earth—big mistake. As a punishment, Warden Zeus chained him to a rock and had a raptor peck at his liver.

Alberta Justice Department officials investigated senior courthouse security officers whose livers were equally anguished, but for a different reason, and whose use of the fire was most unorthodox, engaging as they did in a drunken prank with novices at an Edmonton training school.

The method of instruction was called into question when an officer three three-ply sheets to the wind admitted to dropping his drawers, tucking a length of toilet paper between his arse cheeks and lighting the avant-garde pyrotechnic.

The stunt, performed in front of an audience unluckier than salsa kings at a Mormon social, was inauspiciously videotaped.

A source said this most internal of internal investigations had concluded that the officer's actions constituted violations of government policy, and were inappropriate. And Court and Prisoner Services, which is responsible for courthouse security and hauling prisoners between remand cells and courtrooms, had come under fire in the past for workplace sexual harassment issues.

A witness to the training school episode reported that it occurred in the supervisor's room and that most people attending the instruction facility are aware "a lot of drinking goes on."

The Liberal justice critic, in a most unfortunate reference, accused the then justice minister of "sitting on his hands," but at no point did she mention lighting a metaphorical fire under his ass to deal with an actual one.

Crossing That Thin Blue Line

DAILY NEWS (U.S.), MAY 1995; *HOUSTON CHRONICLE*, MAY 1995; *SAN JOSE MERCURY NEWS*, MAY 1995

Part of the preamble to the 1962 U.S. law that established National Police Week explains the need to recognize police officers for their public service: "Whereas the police officers of America have worked devotedly and selflessly in behalf of the people of this Nation, regardless of the peril or hazard to themselves; and Whereas these officers have safeguarded the lives and property of their fellow Americans ..." Nowhere does the piece of legislation make mention of what an unsuspecting public can do to protect themselves from a crowd of drunk and highly disorderly officers out on a wild bender to mark this special week.

Police from all over the country gathered in Washington in 1995 for National Police Week festivities, including a ceremony led by then president Bill Clinton to honour those who had died in the line of duty. But a contingent of about 200 officers staying at a large hotel, most of them from New York City, spent most of the week pissed out of their trees and terrorizing their fellow guests at area hotels.

An official from the hotel association said that the policemen were "drunk out of their minds" and stayed that way for three days straight.

The unlikely kick-off to the drunken flatfoot fracas was a Saturday-night vigil held to honour deceased officers. Once the vigil was over, around 40 of New York's, ahem, finest got drunk and crazy at their hotel.

Fire alarms began to go off at about 3 A.M., forcing the evacuation of all of the hotel's hundreds of guests, including seniors and the disabled, out of doors. The officers began "spraying fire extinguishers, yelling, singing, screaming and taking their clothes off," according to a hotel staff member, as well as mooning and groping other guests.

The high point of their drunken siege of the hotel occurred when about 20 of the officers poured beer down the central strip of an escalator, took off their clothes and went sliding down in the buff. An employee cleaning the lobby at the time was correct if not somewhat lacking some stronger adjectives when he said: "It was not normal."

Another group of NYPD officers were staying that week at a hotel on Capitol Hill. The officers knocked on hotel doors of attractive women and demanded entry, claiming to be federal agents. Fortunately none of the women obliged the truculent troopers.

Even fellow police officers were not spared the drunken cops' blasted machinations; the emergency-light bar they tore from the roof of a Massachusetts police car was never recovered.

All told, the fatuous flatfoots incurred about $40,000 in damage. Their escapades also led to a public dressing-down by the police commissioner and formal investigations by both their own internal affairs bureau and the Washington Police Department.

Full Monty Morons

THE INDEPENDENT (U.K.), FEBRUARY 1999

The classic image is one of the friendly neighbourhood beat cop taking time out of his day to help a cataract-troubled, little old lady cross a busy road. What little resemblance this image has to reality took a further trouncing at the hands of two policemen and a friend of theirs who were reported to have become drunk and belligerent during a seven-and-a-half-hour flight and to have chosen as outlets for their aggression two elderly female passengers.

The trio comprised a 49-year-old police inspector, his 26-year-old police constable son and their friend, a 56-year-old publican. They were returning to their native Manchester after having had a "fabulous time" on a golfing holiday in Florida.

Not quite ready to kiss the good times goodbye at the 19th hole, the three brought a bottle of gin on to the plane and, after their in-flight drinks had been served, passed the gin between them and proceeded to get sloshed.

The in-flight movie, as twisted fate would have it, was *The Full Monty*. Cabin crew and fellow passengers allege that the two officers and their friend laughed uproariously at the film and at one point got up and began an impromptu mid-air shimmy to go along with the movie—no doubt much to the head-in-hands disgust of the rest of the passengers.

When they saw that two elderly ladies were taking no interest in the comedy about male strippers or their own mid-flight boogie, the trio allegedly turned on them and became abusive, calling the

78-year-old woman, her 71-year-old friend and others "dykes" for not sharing in their merriment.

Despite members of the cabin crew and other passengers recalling this series of events and the pilot having had to come out and speak to the men, the policemen and their friend later denied the allegations.

The police inspector, a man who had been on the job for nearly three decades (and who must have heard far better excuses than the one he came up with), offered no less a ridiculous defence than to say that the women had misinterpreted their comments and that they had been talking about motor "bikes," not "dykes."

In what the presiding judge called a merciful decision, the jury did not hold the dancing cops legally liable for their actions. The judge did not give them costs, however, saying that their behaviour was unbecoming that of police officers.

Cop a Feel, Feel a Cop

DAILY TELEGRAPH (U.K.), JUNE 2002

The policemen's benevolent ball it was not. A £45-a-head charity ball organized by an anti-drugs group in England, meant to honour police and local achievements in the effort to rid the streets of drugs, degenerated into a Bacchanalian orgy of booze and inappropriate behaviour that would have put your local Friday-night abandoned warehouse rave to shame.

The group had staged the benefit in order to raise money as well as give out awards to local businesspeople, police officers and magistrates who had made significant contributions to cutting down on drugs in the streets.

The officers who were set to receive awards at the function were unable to attend, and they seem to have made an unfortunate choice in deciding who should accept the awards in their absence. The group of officers that showed up did so late and drunk, then went on to step over the thin blue line and dance a jig. In the words of one attendee interviewed by the *Daily Telegraph,* "It was absolutely disgusting what they got up to that evening."

Two of the attending officers were groping each other while boogying down on the dance floor, another couple was spotted in a "compromising" position outside and yet one more pair was found exiting a lavatory cubicle after some "county mounty" mounting.

One female officer was said to have hopped up on a banquet table in order, presumably, to give an impromptu tabletop shimmy but fell to the ground before she was able to do so. Another policewoman, perhaps in a lewd homage to Marilyn Monroe in *The Seven Year Itch,* was reported to have danced with her skirt above her head, much to the groping delight of a male colleague near the stage.

The officers involved and their commanding officer faced internal investigations and disciplinary sanctions following the incident. But it wasn't all bad news for the boys in blue. Presumably aided by a high bar bill, the event raised £6,000 for the anti-drugs charity.

The Beer Goggles Effect

A Bausch and Lomb PureVision–funded study carried out by researchers at Manchester University sought to explain why an otherwise discerning person might give out his or her phone number to someone who might be mistaken for a member of a troll family so ugly that they were left by shocked parents on a church doorstep. The researchers' "beer goggles formula" took into account the number of pints consumed, the level of light in the pub or club, the quality of the drinker's own eyesight and the smokiness of the environment. As the effect intensifies, those you might have found "visually offensive" suddenly seem less so, and possibly like a good idea when the bartender yells out last call and all your other options have been exhausted. (BBC, March 2003)

6

Hard Corps Drunks: The Few, the Brave, the Blotto

A man should be upright, not be kept upright.

—Marcus Aurelius

Cock-Eyed and Loaded

The Sun (U.S.), December 2005; *The Scotsman,* December 2005

If you're ever in the decidedly unfortunate situation of running for your life while pursued by an expert marksman—whether it be in the midst of busting out of the joint, taking a stroll through a battlefield or getting off a bus in the wrong neighbourhood— you may think it's to your advantage if the guy who's got you in his sights is seeing double. You'd be wrong. As this story shows, it's usually best for those with their finger on the trigger to be sober.

A sergeant in England found this out for himself when a volley of machine-gun ammo was fired into his leg while he was on duty at the shooting range in his capacity, ironically, as a safety supervisor.

The shooter was a captain who had recently capped off an all-night drinking session.

An insider quoted by *The Sun* said the captain had been up all night drinking with other officers and that the incident occurred "four hours after he swigged his last drop."

After the night's drinking session, the captain had buoyed himself with a two-hour nap and a big mess-hall breakfast before heading off to the shooting range to brush up on his machine-gun skills.

Still feeling a bit wobbly from the previous night's libations, the captain stumbled and the gun went off, firing a round through the sergeant's leg and very nearly putting out of commission this non-commissioned officer. The witness said it was "a miracle" that the sergeant wasn't mowed down by the gunfire, and indeed, as far as errant machine-gun blasts go, the injury from this one was relatively minor, hitting no bones or major organs.

DISHONOURABLE MENTION
Getting Tanked

With technology accelerating rapidly, you no longer have to hold a yard sale and haggle over the price of that chess set with a button substituting for the king with that guy down the street who walks over in his housecoat—not any more, because most sales can now be made quickly and painlessly online. Of course, the sale of some items, such as the one dispatched here, is highly illegal, unethical and even treasonous.

In 1996 Russian troops were disciplined for selling a tank and an armoured combat vehicle following a drunken bender. While this would seem like reason enough to call in the firing squad, the happy new owners of the military hardware were Chechen rebels—a.k.a. the enemy at the time, to those of you who are newspaper averse— with whom the Russian troops had been drinking all day long. There's no word as to whether they hung a sign on the vehicles saying $8,750 (OR BEST OFFER), but that is what the wasted warriors of the motor rifle division received for the hardware. (*Daily Telegraph*, Australia, March 1996)

The Great Curry Battle

THE HERALD (U.K.), FEBRUARY 1992

For a child, the call of "Food fight!" is cause for great excitement— the pulse quickens and strategic positions are taken from which one can comfortably launch a palm-full of mashed potato at Uncle Murray's bald and quickly reddening head. Once you pass the age of, say, 10, however, you realize that among food's many salubrious uses, fashioning it into projectiles to be used in a battle is perhaps the very lowest.

Sadly, not all adults, even the uniformed ones, put aside childish ways, our case in point being a lieutenant commander who capped a night spent in the pubs by joining six of his fellow officers for a meal at an Indian restaurant. The officer was apparently quite out-of-command by the time he reached the restaurant, having downed six pints of beer and one relic of the 1970s, the Harvey Wallbanger cocktail.

At some point during their meal, he took a spoonful of curry and flung it at another officer, thus kicking off masala mayhem. That officer followed suit, and before you could say "hold the chapatti," curry sauce covered the walls and carpet.

Police were summoned to the restaurant; however, the man and some of his officers refused to leave until they had finished eating (what wasn't on the walls). The owner of the restaurant offered to forget the whole thing if the assembled agreed to pay the far-from-exorbitant sum of £20 in damages.

The officer, showing that it is never too late to worsen one's bad behaviour, refused and was subsequently arrested for breach of the peace.

Harvey and the Duke

The Harvey Wallbanger, a staple among the leisure-suit set, was "invented" by famed mixologist Donato "Duke" Antone (also the creator of the Rusty Nail). The story goes that a disconsolate surfer named Harvey popped into Duke's bar after losing an important competition. Duke mixed him one of his "special" screwdrivers to cheer him up. The surfer enjoyed the new mix a little too much; when he tried to leave the bar he kept banging into the walls—and the special screwdrivers were known as Harvey Wallbangers from then on. (Wikipedia.com)

He Shoots, He Singes!

THE SUN (U.K.), DECEMBER 2005

After getting nailed in the face by a puck in 1959, Montreal Canadiens goalie Jacques Plante fashioned a mask for himself and refused to tend goal again without it. The mask has been a part of hockey—and psycho-slasher films—ever since. The move allowed numerous future goaltenders to keep whatever teeth they had left after their time in the junior leagues as well as to offset the disquieting aesthetic effect of "hockey hair."

One can only assume that Plante would have refused outright to join a pickup game of shinny with the lads at one particular military barracks in England. The mask would have provided only a modicum of safety in the version of the game they were playing: "fireball hockey."

A cadet from Royal Military Academy Sandhurst—a prestigious place where Winston Churchill once studied, though that little tidbit is unlikely to be paired with this incident in the institution's public relations literature—visited the Light Dragoons infantry unit. He was considering joining the storied outfit once his training was complete.

On the night of his visit, a black-tie dinner was being held to mark the return of the group from a six-month stint in Iraq. The cadet stayed on and, along with the officers, downed vast quantities of primo wine and brandy.

Once dinner was over, talk turned to recreation, and the officers, displaying the clear-headed thinking that wins wars, decided to head on out to the car park for a game. For those sane people among us who may not be familiar with this extremely dangerous sport, fireball hockey goes by all other hockey rules with one key exception: the "ball" being used is actually a rolled-up wad of tissue paper encased in chicken wire, soaked in lighter fluid and set on fire.

The drunken officers doffed their mess jackets and got into the game, but, as the old saying goes, "It's all fun and games until someone loses an eye," and that very nearly happened. One of the officers hit a powerful slapshot that drilled the cadet right on the forehead, an injury that required a skin graft.

Beware the Smell of a Drunken Sailor
Early in the Mornin'

THE SCOTSMAN, FEBRUARY 1994

Navy men given land privileges for a week or a few days and using that time to get themselves as drunkenly debauched as possible has given us the simile "like a drunken sailor on shore leave." And indeed there is a long history of sailors disembarking from their vessels and letting loose on the port town a hedonistic frenzy that is the delight of barkeeps and bawdy house operators—and the dread of any law-abiding citizen looking for a good night's sleep.

This was the case when a 26-year-old deputy warfare officer received shore leave and went with his mates into a mews in Edinburgh to celebrate. The officer drank nine pints of beer with his shipmates throughout the day and into the evening before disappearing from their sight at some point during the night.

What happened between that point and the next morning, according to the lieutenant's lawyer at his court martial hearing, was due to the young man's weak constitution for alcohol, and the possibility that somebody had spiked one or more of the nine pints he put down that day. He claimed to remember none of what went on.

At around midnight, residents phoned police and reported that a naked man was up to some foul business in the local mews. When police arrived, they found the young lieutenant naked as the day he was born, though considerably more filthy. He had excrement all over his body and had also covered numerous doors in the mews with the same. His clothes were found "soiled and scattered about," according to the prosecuting attorney. Police gave the lieutenant a paper suit to put on while he cleaned up the mess. He was dismissed from his ship over the incident and fined £1,000 for his fecal foray onto shore.

The Joke That Bombed

CBS News, December 2004; Associated Press, December 2004

Since the terrorist incidents of September 11, 2001, most of us know, it is better to err on the side of caution when choosing to make a joke that could cause public alarm. Once upon a time, a grandfather flying to visit his grandson may have elicited a smile or at worst a mild rebuke from a customs official examining his grandson's birthday gift by telling him not to bother, that it's "just a bomb." Nowadays, such a statement is likely to result in the old feller being whisked away to some backroom where he is examined in ways he hasn't been since his military physical.

A civilian may be forgiven for making such a blunder if, say, he has been living in a world cut off from all media for the past 10 years. There is no similar excuse when the offending party is a veteran soldier.

Napoleon must have been howling with laughter in his little grave when a drunken member of a British regiment was arrested after setting off a security alert following a regional costume party to celebrate the regiment's role in the Battle of Waterloo in 1815.

The alarm was due to the soldier's ill-advised choice of costume. He had outfitted himself in a turban, false beard and combat jacket, into which he stuffed wires and candles that were made to look like explosives.

So attired, he set out home along a country road. Someone spotted him and, figuring him for the genuine article, phoned police. Fifteen squad cars arrived on the scene with guns at the ready before realizing that the man was a threat only to good taste.

He spent a night in jail for creating the scare and received a small fine. The presiding judge said that the man received such a light sentence because "there wasn't anything behind his actions. He was just a drunk soldier."

7
Called to the Bar: The Juiced Judiciary

A drunk was in front of a judge. The judge says, "You've been brought here for drinking." The drunk says, "Okay, let's get started."

—HENNY YOUNGMAN

The Case of the Generous Judge

THE INDEPENDENT (U.K.), APRIL 1998; *SEATTLE WEEKLY,* APRIL 1998

Aside from appearing to relish perverting the media's sacred duty to try a case in the court of public opinion, most judges do not seem to display much that resembles human emotion. They slam their gavels all day long, dispatching significant parts of people's lives or fortunes with ease. But in 1998, a Seattle judge took the opportunity to show that judges are just regular people in long flowing black robes (not unlike those in the Sunday crowd at a Moroccan bazaar) when presiding over a DUI case.

The lawyers' ramblings evidently conjured up a bit of a thirst in the judge and, midway through jury deliberation, he left the courtroom and repaired to the local convenience store to buy himself a case of beer.

The judge had polished off a few longnecks by the time the jury returned its verdict. When the entire business was over—no word as to what happened to the DUI defendant, the other enjoyer of tipple in the courtroom—the munificent magistrate invited the lawyers and members of the jury to join him for a drink. Three jurors and a prosecuting attorney partook.

"I bet you never met a judge like me before," he told the four. And, indeed, it was unlikely that they had met anyone like the judge who, witnesses say, drove off that day with a bottle of beer in his hand.

The Commission on Judicial Conduct did not take the judge's impromptu booze-up at all well, later citing him for the incident and forcing his resignation. The judge, a maverick even after the hammer had come down against him, said as he signed his walking papers: "I should have offered them something other than an alcoholic beverage, maybe a Tootsie Pop."

DISHONOURABLE MENTION
Tokyo Rosy Cheeked

Tokyo's labyrinthine public transit system is one of the most efficient and sophisticated on earth, making it easier for a person to get completely lost in that urban setting than virtually anywhere else on the planet. It shuttles nearly 26 million weary souls around town every day, and if that yellowing encyclopedia in the basement closet is correct, that's roughly half the population of the entire country.

A Tokyo District judge, who had been presiding over a golf course investment case and whose eyes, surprisingly, had glazed over not from the tedious details of the proceedings but from partying it up the night before, fell asleep on a subway. His attaché containing important legal documents related to the case was snatched from him as he slept, which resulted in what was, we're sure, an embarrassing delay of court proceedings.

The judge's frustration at being robbed likely did not match the disappointment of the thief, who, when comparing that day's haul with that of his subway-robbing cronies, was likely shamed that in lieu of cold hard cash or a sellable laptop, he found himself with a stack of legal documents. (*Daily Yomiuri,* April 1993)

Vital and Not So Vital Fluids

New Zealand Herald, November 2004

Olympians, porn stars and professional athletes may be well versed in asking strange favours; however, in other professions the need to befriend someone who will, say, pee in a cup on your behalf very rarely, if ever, arises.

One would assume that those sitting in judgment over others would know better than to try to mess around with such matters, but an Australian judge got into trouble for doing just that, attempting to eliminate physical evidence that could have proved damaging in a court of law.

The judge had driven his car into one of those pesky stationary vehicles that always seem to spring out of nowhere, and he was brought to hospital shortly after midnight by a concerned friend.

Staff, noticing that the good judge reeked to high heaven of alcohol, took a sample of his blood.

According to inquiry lawyers, the gavel-banger then absconded with his own plasma sample from a hospital trolley, thus attempting to pervert the course of justice. If convicted, the judge would have faced up to 14 years' imprisonment. It wasn't until the mounting political strain built up like his blood pressure that the judge caved, conceding that he had the sample in his possession. He then handed the evidence over to authorities.

The Prosecutor Rests His Case (of Beer)

THE MIRROR (U.K.), AUGUST 2004;
SOUTH CHINA MORNING POST, AUGUST 2004

Going to trial is never a pleasant experience. No matter how nicely ironed your suit is or how otherwise attractive your appearance, there is still a chance at the end of the day that you could be sent to a place where they ladle stew into tin bowls and where being able to fashion your toothbrush into a deadly weapon is seen as a marketable skill.

The prosecuting attorney is the one bent on sending you there; however, if you ever find yourself in the defendant's dock you may get lucky and have someone like the star of this tale arguing the merits of the state's case against you.

Actually, the British barrister in question here won the case, in which he was trying a group convicted of cigarette smuggling, in a Hong Kong court and only made his newspaper-headline-grabbing display during the sentencing phase of the trial.

Returning to the hearing from a lunchtime adjournment, the barrister was wearing sunglasses (never a good sign for a man working indoors), appeared unsteady on his feet and stank of booze. As the judge read his summation, the libation-filled lawyer giggled and tapped his fingers on his desk, and when the magistrate congratulated one of the co-defendants on beating drug addiction, the lawyer applauded.

Frustrated by the lawyer's outbursts (and the fact that he was cheering for the wrong side), the judge adjourned the hearing again so that the drunken counsel could "control himself."

The lawyer, however, did not limit his antics to the courtroom. He went on to make some permanent friends in the local press by standing outside the halls of justice and posing as Rodin's *The Thinker* while photographers happily snapped away.

He later admitted to having been as "drunk as a monkey" during the trial on two dry martinis and several beers, and was later suspended.

Your Honour Is into His Cups

THE PROVINCE (CANADA), MARCH 1992

Volleyball is like dodge ball, a game whose object is to elicit red welts on your opponent's backside and give the more popular kids in school a chance to spike a rock-hard piece of synthetic leather pumped full of compressed air into the faces of their decidedly less popular classmates.

The sport of volleyball requires that players concentrate on their spikes, bumps and sets, as well as the concomitant burning sensation in the forearms, in order to be successful. In the annals of sports-team antics, not even a fire set in the phys-ed building, a horrible gym rash or that rapscallion Travis mooning his red-faced classmates would be as off-putting as the sight to which a visiting girls' volleyball team was exposed while staying at a hotel in Newfoundland.

A provincial court heard that a federal court judge was spotted by team members cavorting about in the hotel hallway clad in a black bra, panties and nylons—one can only assume he chose the colour of his skivvies to match the sombre garb he dons in the court-room. The hotel's general manager was summoned to deal with the juiced judge.

Defence counsel said that while the girls were exposed to a most unsettling sight, the judge did not expose himself or make any sort of perverted advance toward the girls, and that his Carnaval in Rio–like choice of attire was a trivial matter and "clearly alcohol-related."

Rather than face for the rest of his career on the bench the court-room conjecture as to what exactly was under his robes, the judge took an early retirement for medical reasons, for which he would receive a full pension of $98,000 a year—plenty of scratch to keep himself ensconced in the finest La Perla bloomers.

No Kidding, Eh?

Residents of the province of Newfoundland and Labrador are the highest per-capita consumers of beer, wine and spirits in Canada. (Stats Canada, 2004)

Losing Streak

St. Petersburg Times (U.S.), February 2005

Streaking hit its peak during the 1970s when hairy people seemed to spring from the woodwork eager to drop their drawers and run amok in a public place in the hope of shocking others. Booze has, not surprisingly, played an important role in many of these events, giving people the inhibition reduction needed for them to want to inflict their naked selves on others.

A prosecutor in Florida added his own chapter to the book of streakerdom more recently. He had spent a day partying it up with his buddies at a Florida motel—wait, it gets tackier—when he decided at one point that it would be the height of hilarity if he stripped buck naked and hid in the back seat of what he thought was his buddy's vehicle.

Unfortunately for him, the person in the driver's seat was not one of his larrikin buddies but rather a woman who was sitting there waiting for her boyfriend. The full-frontal view in her rear-view mirror was too much for the woman, who began to scream, and called 911 on her cell phone.

Police found the prankster prosecutor drunk and naked in the middle of the parking lot.

He was presumably back in his best barrister's attire when charges were read to him of disorderly intoxication and indecent exposure.

Drunk Juror Furor

ST. LOUIS POST–DISPATCH, MARCH 1991

Claiming a bad back is a great way to get out of work. Much like feigning deafness in one ear (or both, if you're ambitious) to get out of military service, this is an effective, if more provisional, way to avoid that next board meeting/presentation/office power-lunch. The beauty of a bad back is that it can resolve on its own immediately, or take a few days—a short enough time that one does not have to justify stretching the truth about having seen a doctor.

Less effective is saying you overslept, because it implies idleness and sloth even if you say, for example, that your alarm didn't go off or your electricity was shorted out by that guy running a marijuana grow-op in your basement.

Unfortunately, sleeping in was the best excuse a St. Louis man sitting on a jury for a murder trial could come up with after he missed a day of deliberations.

The jury had deliberated for four hours on the previous night, and had been sent home by the judge with instructions to return at 9 A.M. sharp the next day. Rather than following the judge's instructions, the juror went to a friend's house and set out on pounding back the rather unorthodox combination of gin and beer.

Defending his actions later, the juror said that he had become so depressed at hearing the testimony during the trial, which involved a fatal shooting and a love triangle, that he decided to get drunk at his friend's place, and thus ended up oversleeping. Actually, that's an understatement by most people's definition of the word. While the defendant's fate hung in the balance, the juror slept for most of the day, missing the trial by a good nine hours.

Police were even dispatched to go look for the no-show, and it was finally decided, with the permission of the accused, to proceed without him and go with an 11-member jury.

For missing the final deliberations of the murder case, the indolent juror got his own mini-trial and was sentenced to contempt of court and fined $700. Now, there's a wake-up call.

8

Doctors Feelgood and Other Health-Care Hijinks

I'd rather have a bottle in front of me, than a frontal lobotomy.

—ANONYMOUS

Doctor Feel-No-Pain

OTTAWA CITIZEN, APRIL 1997; *DAILY TELEGRAPH* (U.K.), APRIL 1997; *BRITISH MEDICAL JOURNAL,* APRIL 1997

It's a dilemma that every adoptive parent must face one day: whether to tell your 8-foot red-headed NBA forward son that you, the albino circus-dwarf couple who raised him, are not in fact his natural parents. If you decide to reveal all, the telling of it requires a delicate touch—explaining to him that you always loved him as your own, giving him a basic outline of genetics and asking him why he didn't clue in earlier. What you don't need is some drunken punter spilling the beans.

One family's most guarded secret regarding their children's origins came to be known in just this manner at their pub in the United Kingdom.

The pub owners were away on holiday when the good doctor, having knocked back five pints of Guinness, chose to disclose loudly for all to hear that the vacationing couple conceived their two youngest children through artificial insemination. One of those within earshot was the couple's 17-year-old daughter, who had had no idea that her younger brother and sister were conceived in this manner. She burst into tears upon hearing the news and later demanded to know why her parents hadn't told her.

The couple ended up moving as a result of the doctor's spontaneous revelation, saying that they could no longer face the crowd at their local watering hole. The doctor's loose lips around the beer-nut set led him to be found guilty of serious professional misconduct by the General Medical Council, a decidedly more sober group.

Good for What Ales Ya

The fastest pint of stout was consumed by Peter Dowdeswell, who slugged back a pint of Guinness in just 2.1 seconds at the Millwall Football Club in London on April 24, 2001, according to the *Guinness Book of World Records*—and they should know.

Who Was That Drunken Masked Man?

THE ARGUS (U.S.), MARCH 2006; *THE SCOTSMAN*, MARCH 2006

As anyone who's ever lingered in a doctor's waiting room knows, the process can be gruelling. While thumbing through months-old copies of *Reader's Digest* and having a colicky baby dribbling green goo on the sleeve of your best sweater, the mind wanders to a cost–benefit assessment of curing that mysterious rash.

A California neurosurgeon, unaccustomed to having to wait around for a few hours like any patient and likely fearing that it would cut into his tee time, threw a drunken fit after being told he couldn't operate on a spinal fracture patient immediately. He was told, in what was probably a stalling tactic to get the drunk and disorderly doctor a safe distance from the patient, that he would have to wait for surgical instruments and implants to be properly sterilized.

The surgeon, according to a witness, exclaimed, "Do you know that I am a [expletive] doctor, and I'm going to do what I want?" as he threatened a nurse who had refused to assist in the procedure until the equipment was disinfected.

The doctor told the nurse that he wasn't interested in hospital procedure and, loosing another expletive, said that if he did not perform the surgery immediately the patient "would lose his life," this despite having consulted with two sober surgeons who said the man's life was not in danger.

When staff alerted the police, the surly sawbones took a swing at them and was promptly arrested. Deputies in the emergency room melee had to wrestle the doctor to the ground to handcuff him— presumably taking care not to injure the surgeon's healing, albeit at that point unsteady, hands.

Drinking Emergency

DAILY TELEGRAPH (U.K.), JANUARY 2006

Generally when one has need of an ambulance, any wait time seems too long, what with the minutes stretching out the way they do when a serious injury, poisoning or other potential cause of death is at hand. When you dial 911 you assume that all emergency response vehicles are ready to be employed, or are in use, but not in the manner they were in this case.

In the United Kingdom, 15 merry medics, doctors and nurses, decked out in civilian attire rather than their scrubs, courted what could have been an uncomfortable stomach pumping from their work-bound colleagues by quaffing copious birthday libations including bottles of champagne, shots of sambuca, pints and wine at the local tavern.

A bartender asked them if they wanted him to call a taxi, but one of the group told him not to bother, that they had one coming.

When their "taxi," or ambulance, as it is known to those about to shuffle off their mortal coil, arrived at 11 P.M., the group of them piled into the back of it.

The medical personnel faced disciplinary action, and the ambulance service later issued an apology, stressing that patient services were not compromised that night because the vehicle used for the group's bender was at the time returning to its base.

Other pub-goers said the incident was "shocking" considering the £30-million deficit faced by the local hospital trust. More shocking was that these well-paid health-care professionals were too cheap to pony up for a cab.

DISHONOURABLE MENTION
Careless Home Care

A health board in Ireland investigated a home-care physician whose conduct was most definitely subpar. For a start, the doctor, who was standing in for an on-leave GP, didn't bother to encumber himself with minor details like updated medical malpractice insurance ("So I *don't* have malpractice insurance—sue me!").

The physician missed a morning visit, and when he showed up in the evening he was, in the patient's family's words, "drunk and abusive," unquestionably as a result of the medic's unconventional repast: oysters washed back with lots of Guinness.

The drunken doctor went on to slump across his patient's bed in the middle of the examination.

The inquiry later made the wild suggestion that temporary doctors actually get their own registration and medical insurance. (*Irish Independent,* March 2006)

This Will Only Hurt a Bit (Hiccup)

BBC, JUNE 2004; *THE SUN* (U.K.), JUNE 2004

A visit to the dentist is one of the rare times you get an up-close view of the unsightly inner workings of your own mouth and, if you live on a busy person's diet of Coca-Cola and chocolate bars, a great deal of intense pain. The situation is unpleasant enough under normal circumstances, but if the professional poking around in your mouth with those sharp metal instruments is intoxicated, as a woman in England found out, things can get a whole lot worse.

Her consultation, which began after lunch, involved a routine extraction, for which most of the pain occurs once the anaesthetic has worn off. Unbeknownst to his patient, however, the drunken dentist had enjoyed six glasses of wine during his lunch hour, which had obliterated the fine motor skills needed to carry out his work.

After two unsuccessful stabs at injecting the anaesthetic into her gum, he set about with the extraction before the painkiller had a chance to take effect. The woman in the chair, quite naturally, began to scream in agony. She said that after much shouting and pain, the doctor, sweating and stinking of booze, slumped over her and began to shake.

The patient called it the "most terrifying" experience of her life. In addition to botching the extraction, the drunken dentist had broken one of the woman's good teeth. Another dentist, presumably one on the wagon during working hours, was brought in to finish the original extraction as well as to take out the tooth that the drunken dentist had broken.

The dentist in question was professionally censured over the incident, and as for his poor patient, she requires another visit—though she said that after that horrific experience, she will have trouble going to the dentist ever again.

Good Night, Nurse!

THE SCOTSMAN, OCTOBER 1999; *THE INDEPENDENT* (U.K.), OCTOBER 1999

When you're stuck in a hospital bed for any length of time, your only hope of comfort rests with a kind nurse, one who will tend to you by gently administering potent painkillers on a frequent basis, giving you sponge baths and patiently listening to every complaint you can think of since her last visit. At the very least, you will most likely want the people responsible for dispensing your medications, managing your IV drip and poking you with a dozen potentially very painful needles to be able to walk a straight line and touch index finger to nose without much trouble if called on to do so.

A U.K. nursing council dismissed a 47-year-old relief nurse in Scotland for making her rounds on a ward full of elderly patients while heavily under the influence.

The nurse had been called in to provide relief due to a staff shortage at the hospital; however, the typically reliable nurse was on this day only capable of providing (and even this depends on your sense of humour) comic relief.

The elderly patients on the ward were exposed to behaviour that would have sent any bedpan a mile high in shock. According to *The Scotsman,* staff reported to the nursing council that rather than walking around the ward, she "bounced," that she repeatedly went into the wrong wards, and that she did not notice when the nasal drip of one of her patients had run out. And in what, purely on the conjecture of the authors, might have put a rainbow on an otherwise drab day for some old cacker, she also was reported to have "sat on a bed in an over-familiar manner with a patient."

The nurse was escorted off hospital premises once it had been determined that she, unlike her patients, was feeling no pain. She later issued a shame-filled unconditional apology for the incident.

III

Crime Doesn't Pay (Your Bar Tab)

Criminology has come a long way from the time when temples and foreheads were probed for telltale cranial lumps believed to indicate good breeding, predisposition to felony, a virtuous nature or an IQ that relegated the individual to menial tasks usually reserved for the town mule. Today we know that biology alone does not determine criminal nature—a source of relief for those whose families are full of more bad apples than an orchard hit by frost.

Why some people turn to a life of crime and others to a life of, say, horticulture, is an unanswerable mystery best left to the capable hands of the guys who write murder-mystery dinner theatre. What we're trying to illustrate in Crime Doesn't Pay (Your Bar Tab) is merely what happens when the world of crime—a most disorganized one in this case—mixes with heavy boozing, and we're not talking about mafia types enjoying a nice dollop of postprandial grappa to commemorate that "most unfortunate accident" that befell Dominick "The Chin" Delvecchio.

These are not the sleek enemies of the law that make up for the block-of-wood protagonist in action movies. Films featuring these criminals would be decidedly short and one-sided.

For some, a night in the drunk-tank spent with some psychopath whispering about how he could strangle a man with his shoelaces if they hadn't been confiscated is all the punishment they receive. In the Jailhouse Now chronicles those whose drunken exploits were often the cause of their facing hard time.

Though the old saying "Crime doesn't pay" might not apply to someone living off its largesse in a penthouse suite with a more sizable retinue on hand than that of the Prince of Wales, it most certainly applies to the unfortunates featured in this section. Crime doesn't pay well at all when you're half-crocked.

9

From the Still to the Till: Thieving Drunks

If once a man indulges himself in murder, very soon he comes to think little of robbing; and from robbing he comes next to drinking and Sabbath-breaking, and from that to incivility and procrastination.

—THOMAS DE QUINCEY

Where the Buffalonian Roamed

BUFFALO NEWS, APRIL 2001

Exploding dye is a hazard—not only for thieving acne-addled teens trying to shove Gap T-shirts into their backpacks and avoid the Barney Fife mall-security guards, but also for modern-day Robbin' Hoods who admirably attempt to avoid the 9-to-5 workaday grind by jacking up big banks for a living. It's fitting that they're called "holdups" because, as anyone trying to cash that $12 Christmas cheque from grandma on their lunch hour knows, you're often held up for an extended period of time, waiting for the next available teller who's busy changing someone's 200 bucks into its equivalent in Hungarian forint. Admit it—anyone who has ever been dinged with a $2 service charge at the bank machine secretly sides with the likes of old-time bank-robbing heroes like John Dillinger or Bonnie and Clyde.

While John Dillinger became a folk anti-hero for the grace he displayed when committing his robberies—the sleek way he would leap over a bank counter to elude police in the nick of time—the same cannot be said for one Buffalo bandit. Unlike his predecessors, who were brought down in a haze of bullets, this man's arrest was due to his drink-filled haze at the time of the crime.

The bandit, referred to rather uncharitably by a state prosecutor and his own attorney as the "town drunk," was living up to his appellation on the day he walked into a bank intoxicated and demanded money from a clerk. He even went so far as to threaten to "shoot" if he wasn't given the cash, even though the gun in question comprised his thumb and forefinger.

The clerk handed him the requested cash, but unbeknownst to the robber, gave it to him in a red dye pack that was set to explode—and did, shortly after he left the scene.

Undeterred, he continued on to his local tavern, which was truly local in that it was about 100 yards from the bank. Covered in red ink, and passing dyed-red notes, the effusive robber announced that today the drinks were on him—a rare treat from such a local personality, as anyone familiar with town drunks will know.

Alas, it didn't take police officials long to walk the 100 yards separating the bar from the bank, nor to decide that the man covered in red dye from the exploding pack was probably their chief suspect.

The Bar Thief Who Couldn't Say No

Jerusalem Post, November 2005

To burgle well requires some grace. Indeed the term *cat burglar* refers to the need to exhibit feline stealth and light-footedness when committing a burglary. Crash into Aunt Gertie's rich estate like a falling-down-drunk bull in a china shop and you're likely to have large dogs at your throat before you even have a chance to think about the old gal's precious-stones collection.

An Israeli burglar displayed no grace or finesse whatsoever and could have used a few lessons in the art of successful looting. The main lesson: when committing a burglary in a bar, do not hinder your chances for escape by liberally sampling the goods.

The bar had been closed for a couple of hours when the burglar broke in—immediately triggering the security alarm. Failing to prepare for such an occurrence was enough of a blunder, but the man also failed to realize that no business operated by anybody with any sense whatsoever keeps the previous day's earnings in the till overnight.

The burglar found the equivalent of US$149 in the till, just enough cash for employees to get started the next day. Not satisfied with this meagre haul, he instead decided to take payment in kind, pulling a bottle of booze down and getting sloppy drunk. By the time police arrived, they found the bombed burglar passed out on one of the bar's couches.

When they roused him, he told the police he had just been napping and would be on his way now.

Waltzing Away with a Masterpiece

SYDNEY MORNING HERALD, MAY 2003;

THE ADVERTISER (AUSTRALIA), JANUARY 2006; ANSWERS.COM

Retailers rely on the impulsivity of consumers. They exploit our need for instant gratification by lining up fattening, sugary treats, which we might not ordinarily purchase, barring insulin shock, right at the checkout. As you decide you want to learn more about how Oprah was abducted by aliens then promptly returned to earth by her baffled captors, and throw in some Hershey products to gnaw on while you read, you are making what marketing geniuses refer to as "the impulse buy."

Businesses around the world make hundreds of millions of dollars yearly through impulse buys, and while we don't have the specific accounting on hand to prove it, we can only imagine that being drunk significantly increases one's impulsivity.

A Viennese native, or "Weiner" (cue juvenile giggling), behind the theft of the world's most valuable sculpture from Vienna's Art History Museum, made the heist, he said, on a spur-of-the-moment impulse hastened by drink. *Saliera,* a 16th-century sculpture by Florentine master Benvenuto Cellini, rendered in ivory, gold and vitreous enamel, and to our eyes incredibly tacky (but a different, 500-year-old kind of tacky), is valued at more than US$80 million.

Investigators scoured the globe for the stolen piece, and eventually their investigation closed in on, of all people, a security alarm installer. As people in his line of work would, he noticed that there was a builder's scaffolding outside of the museum and that the windows did not have alarms.

One night while drunk, the 50-year-old decided to break in and, on an impulse, make off with the late-Renaissance sculpture. While investigators searched desperately for the missing masterpiece, it remained under the security alarm installer's bed in his Viennese flat for a year and a half before he buried it in a box in a forest outside the city.

When investigators had his photo published, the impulsive klepto came forward and led them to the place where he had buried the statue, a gaudy piece of work that would not look out of place being spit-shined by a cathouse madam.

Hair of the Dog-Day Afternoon

THE INDEPENDENT (U.K.), DECEMBER 1992

Plucking up one's courage for an act that is likely to be hard on the nerves by quaffing an alcoholic beverage or two is a common enough practice. Who among us, when about to break off a relationship or do a dine-and-dash at a slow-service restaurant, for example, hasn't fortified ourselves beforehand with a couple of belts of the old nectar?

It is an inadvisable course of action to take, however, when you are in the midst of committing a crime, such as robbing a bank, in which one misstep could land you in a federal penitentiary. Two London bank robbers, surprisingly, were able to carry out four successful heists despite a fondness for the drink.

Detesting violence, the pair concocted an M.O. whereby they could commit their robberies without having to shed any blood. According to the plan, one perp would enter the bank first, posing as an ordinary customer. The other would then enter and pretend to take his buddy hostage at knifepoint, threatening to cut his throat if the requested money was not produced.

To work up the daring to carry off this piece of performance art, the bank robbers figured they required strong drink to steady their nerves. On one occasion this resulted in the would-be hostage getting so drunk prior to the robbery that he passed out, outside of the target bank.

His "captor," probably thinking that the show must go on, picked the man up and dragged him into the bank, still continuing the hostage ruse and, amazingly, getting away with it—to the tune of £2,330. The "hostage" was arrested shortly thereafter, and told police that he had no memory whatsoever of that particular heist.

His partner, meanwhile, found a replacement for him and went on to commit one additional robbery before he too was nabbed.

DISHONOURABLE MENTION
Cottage Cheesy Caper

A typical portable television is roughly 15 inches or less. Anything more and its "portability" is debatable, but what is unequivocal is that these are great devices to lug to the cottage in order to catch a rabbit-ear antennae repeat of *Matlock* in between the patio beer-quaffing, fly-swatting and Lyme-disease avoidance. Be careful when furnishing your home in the woods, though, to choose the cheapest junk you can find, so that no one would ever want to steal it.

Police in Leamington, Ontario, were called to the scene of a robbery in which a 25-year-old man had attempted a raid on a cottage but got too drunk to properly carry it off. The man was found in a "heavily intoxicated condition," passed out beside an overturned bicycle, the getaway vehicle of choice for the law-breaking, lethargic Tour de France cast-off. A television that might have been too much for him to lug was found at the end of the driveway, and next to him was a bag containing more cottage contraband.

Four additional suspects were charged in connection with the heist, likely because one man alone couldn't possibly have masterminded such a sophisticated criminal caper. (*Windsor Star,* August 2004)

Has Anybody Seen This Saint?

TORONTO STAR, JUNE 1988; ABC NEWS, FEBRUARY 2006

Nowadays on eBay, you can procure a strand of Elvis's hair set in a spiffy custom frame. If movies have taught us anything, and they most certainly have, it's that in the future men in white coats will use such anatomical parts to clone The King, who will come back to re-popularize sequinned jumpsuits, grease-exclusive diets and the shag carpeting on one's living room walls as an interior design statement.

Presumably, once all the A-list celebrities like Elvis are cloned, scientists can then move on to lesser-known lights like the 19th-century French saint in this story, Bernadette. Short of raiding the saint's tomb in Nevers, France, however, finding a suitable piece of genetic material will now prove difficult thanks to the antics of a couple of drunk Canadian college kids out on a lark. They broke into a Winnipeg church and stole not only a cheap plastic knock-off of the saint, but an actual lock of her hair.

A nun at the church said the drunken pair later offered to replace the plastic-and-cloth statue of St. Bernadette, adding that they had no clue as to its whereabouts or that of the saint's hair, given that they were completely trashed at the time of the theft.

The men told the sister that they had been on a three-day drinking binge and that by the time they happened upon the church they did not even know where they were. It seems unlikely, therefore, that they'll ever find their way to France to get their hands on a replacement lock of hair.

Incidentally, St. Bernadette is believed to have seen the Virgin Mary appear on 18 occasions (36 if she'd been drinking heavily).

DISHONOURABLE MENTION
Compliments of the House

The words "this round's on me" are music to the ears of every barfly; however, before you announce to the world that you have just made a new best friend, it is best to take note of whether your drinking companion is behaving strangely or wearing a balaclava—or a Richard Nixon mask as the case may be.

In Australia, a thirsty drunk rambled into a pub after hours and asked for a pint, not realizing that two thieves were busy robbing the place. The obliging bandits poured him three drinks, and hung around with the man until the booze overcame him and he fell asleep.

The thieves then raided the pub's safe, making off with all its valuables and expensive stereo equipment.

When the drunkard awoke to police questioning, he wasn't much help, describing them as "one big bloke and one smaller one." (*Morning Advertiser,* Australia; Ananova.com, U.K., April 2006)

Half-Baked Robbery

DAILY TELEGRAPH (AUSTRALIA), MARCH 1996

The biggest crime when it comes to bread is that in less-than-reputable dining establishments, it's rumoured that if you ask for more they just grab unused portions from other patrons who haven't touched theirs (after a perfunctory whisking of the baguettes into the kitchen, where they're retouched to look like they're making their dining room debut). While disgusting, this is not a bookable offence. An Australian man's use of bread, on the other hand, was.

Early one morning, an Australian thief well into his cups entered a 7-Eleven, selected a chocolate bar from his unconventional arsenal and, waving it at the store manager, demanded $50.

After his request was rejected by the manager, and possibly after having seen one too many Monty Python sketches, the buzzed but undeterred burglar marched behind the counter, where he unsheathed a baguette. He swung it at the manager, who wisely locked up the register and ran outside.

Turns out it was the burglar's birthday, and he had presumably decided to mark the occasion in the time-honoured tradition of blowing out birthday candles, opening gifts and chasing a convenience store manager around a parking lot with a breadstick, shouting: "If you don't give me the money I'll kill you."

The foiled crusader, still brandishing his baked weaponry, demanded money from a taxi driver before heading back inside the store to search for hard cash.

Witnesses flagged down the police, who gave chase. No word on whether the attacker tried to eat the evidence.

Beats a Bread Stick

A Worcester, Massachusetts, man who was tossed out of a pub returned with a friend armed with an unorthodox choice of weaponry—a samurai sword, which he swung at the bartender. (CourtTV.com, April 2006)

Sleeping with the (Drunken) Enemy

THE PRESS (NEW ZEALAND), DECEMBER 2003

There are certain things that nobody wants to wake up to: blaring police sirens, the music of Ted Nugent, or a *National Geographic* alarm clock that plays a recording of a macaque's shriek. Certainly, though, any of these three would be preferable to waking up as one couple in New Zealand did, to a naked drunken man who has just robbed you—and is now in your bed.

The intruder, a 28-year-old German, broke into the married couple's apartment through their bathroom window after they had already fallen asleep. While skulking around their apartment he came across a bottle of whisky, and, recognizing it as primo aged stuff, proceeded to polish off half.

Quite drunk by this point and in need of release, his second order of business was to do his business in the couple's bathroom. Duly relieved, and apparently not one to be restricted by cumbersome clothing, the drunken burglar then stripped and had a look around for the bedroom. He was undaunted by the fact that the bed was already occupied, lay down next to the couple and was quickly off to the land of Nod.

The couple slept on unknowingly—that is, until the burglar began to snore. They sprang up and immediately phoned police, who arrived and threw a blanket over the still-sleeping drunk before arresting him.

DISHONOURABLE MENTION
Next Stop: Jail

In Toronto, a careless bank robber was so jiggered that he inadvertently added his plunder to a public transit lost-and-found. The thief, after robbing a bank on Yonge Street (which, at nearly 1,250 miles is known as the longest street in the world, and to Torontonians as "that street downtown with all the strip clubs"), accidentally left the filthy lucre in a sweater on the subway.

The District Court sentenced the man to nine months' probation—and there was no word if his transit pass was revoked. (*Toronto Star,* January 1986)

Lots of Luck (and All of It Bad)
St. Louis Post–Dispatch, March 1990

Successful criminals, i.e., the ones not telling you their stories through Plexiglas, must have a bit of luck on their side in order to get things done. When luck is against you, carrying off a crime can be difficult, and when it is *extraordinarily* against you, as it was in the case of this poor sucker, then it's best that you are at least sober when you give your statement at police headquarters.

One Missouri native was having problems with his girlfriend, and dealt with these troubled waters by sitting down and having a reasonable discussion with her over coffee—just kidding: by drinking his face off. Drunk and feeling wronged by his woman, the broken-hearted boozer started off his ill-fated mini crime spree by stealing a car. His luck in that was no better than in his relationships, because he ended up crashing the car.

A passing motorist gave the man a lift into town and after dropping him off, having sensed something amiss (we're guessing the sight of blood and the smell of booze), called the police.

Not content to call it a day after that debacle, the car thief then decided to add a breaking-and-entering rap to his record by busting into a hardware store. This was not the best move, as hardware stores—unlike, say, a jewellery store or a store specializing in Fabergé eggs—do not lend themselves to the same sort of light "crash in and carry off" type of robbery. He made his exit more prepared to spackle his bathroom than to go on the lam, carrying 13 bucks' worth of utility knives, a broad knife and a putty knife.

Perhaps feeling a bit gutted at his pitiful loot, the drunken car thief/burglar then went to flag down a ride home. The first car to make its way over the hill, as those of you whose neurons are still firing already may have guessed, was a police cruiser—the one responding to the call made by the man who earlier had given the thief a ride.

The drunken burglar stopped waving immediately and tried to make his getaway, but to no avail. What little threads his defence might have hung on were severed completely when his cache of loot from the hardware store fell onto the floor of the police cruiser.

DISHONOURABLE MENTION
Short-Sighted Move

A London, Ontario, man with a 150-proof drinking problem and a history of more than 100 convictions was sentenced to six months in jail after pleading guilty to robbing a charity for the blind-drunk, er, blind. A coin-donation box was swiped from a restaurant counter and the tactless and intoxicated thief was seen pocketing 21 bucks in change. (*London Free Press,* Canada, March 2006)

10
In the Jailhouse Now:
Big House—Worthy Benders

I don't like jail, they got the wrong kind of bars in there.

—CHARLES BUKOWSKI

Not Dealing with a Full Deck

BBC News Online, January 2000; *The Scotsman*, May 2000;
Irish Emigrant News, February 2005

Dealing drugs successfully is all about keeping cool. The last thing you want to do when you plan on ending the day by crapping out a balloon full of contraband is to draw attention to yourself. It is best to blend into the crowd by dressing in neutral colours and avoiding conversation—or, if you are forced into one, chattering about football, where to get the best fish and chips and how unusually blustery the weather is for this time of year.

A drug mule from Northern Ireland was planning to smuggle a whopping 50,000 tablets of ecstasy from a port town to his home country. On the evening prior to the scheduled delivery, however, he decided to meet up with a drug dealer in the area, stash his haul (worth approximately £500,000) at his guesthouse and join said drug dealer on a bender.

In a scene reminiscent of an Irvine Welsh novel, the pair went on a pub crawl and got smashed, whereupon the drug mule proceeded to proclaim loudly what he had stashed away in his room. Hearing that, the proprietor of the bar kicked them out, and the pair returned to their lodgings.

Back at the guesthouse the drunken duo continued their baffling attention-grabbing antics by climbing up on the roof, spooking the manager's wife and again getting kicked out, this time with their stash.

As if they hadn't done enough to attract attention to themselves, the pair took off and at some point decided to park their minivan— at an angle that would inspire Pythagoras. A policeman took note of the skewed vehicle and his suspicions rose further when the drug mule walked up to it, hesitated and then walked off.

The officer approached the vehicle and looked inside to see if there was anything to identify the owner. Opening the rear hatch to the van, the officer found a heavy rucksack. Anti-terror measures, including a sniffer dog, were called in before it was determined that the sack was actually full of thousands of happy-dance pills.

In a sorry addendum to this tale, one month after serving four years for the above crime, the mule was arrested again on a similar charge.

The Beer Hunter

TORONTO STAR, JUNE 1989

As any seasoned outdoorsman knows, hunting with an assault rifle is the most humane way of dispatching Bambis. Like some backwoods Travis Bickle, you can go Malthusian on these woodland invaders, letting the rounds fly with your gas-operated, rotating-bolt Kalashnikov, or, if mowing down fauna at 1,200 feet doesn't give you a case of the Henry David Thoreau touchy-feelies, you can always get your hands dirty by strapping on the bayonet-knife and doing the deed up close.

Unlike most hunters, who head out into the hinterlands, down a case of Pabst Blue Ribbon around a fireplace and stagger into the woods smelling blood, one 39-year-old hunter, presumably unable to stomach the great outdoors, went hunting for prey of the two-legged variety in suburban Toronto.

The ripped rifleman showed up in front of a suburban home and exposed himself to the residents, an activity made all the more awkward by the fact that he knew some of them. Perhaps to break the uncomfortable silence, he discharged his piece, forcing the occupants to dive for cover. Six of the shots passed through the wall while the other bullets whizzed close to a woman on a sofa.

The man then got into his truck and promptly crashed into a utility pole. Seeing that the pole was leaning at a precarious angle, he attempted to finish the job—with an axe.

After saying that society could not tolerate this type of behaviour, the judge in this case threw the book at the fellow, and missed widely—giving him a 90-day sentence to be served on weekends so that he could continue to cavort with the criminal underbelly of society in his job as a roofer.

This Is a Stick-up! (Just Kidding)

PRESS ASSOCIATION (U.K.), OCTOBER 2000

Post-traumatic stress disorder can result from a variety of experiences, usually those in which one is threatened with death, bodily harm or being forced to pick up a hefty tab at a restaurant. To get over such episodes you need to relax by doing things like soaking in long hot baths and babbling ad nauseum to a professional paid to listen to you—or, if the fees charged by such a professional are too exorbitant, a bartender.

If, heaven forbid, your recovery is marred by a *repeat* of the same anxiety- and stress-inducing episode, your final nerve might very well snap and you could end up at a "laughing academy" wearing shoes with no laces.

Staff at a credit union in southern England were traumatized when an armed raid was carried out there, and some of them took time off afterwards to recover from the emotional stress of the episode. They had just returned to work after their leave and were attempting to get back to their day-to-day routines when a couple of men waltzed into the building drunk and out to play a grievously ill-timed prank.

The pair was just pretending to rob the place, but their "playful" demands of money from the cashier were taken seriously by the shell-shocked staff. Satisfied that they'd pulled off their hoax, the two left empty-handed, and were found later in the day downing sherry on a nearby street.

In defending the pair, their lawyer said that they were a couple of drunks who had behaved poorly but who were harmless when sober.

The drunken duo was arrested for the faux robbery and sentenced to six months' imprisonment on charges of affray, for causing extreme terror to the credit union. With such a heavy punishment (and admittedly, this is editorializing on the part of the authors), they might as well have gone ahead and robbed the place for real.

Sammy the Bear's Last Hurrah

Sunday Mail (U.K.), January 2006

Topping a list of shank-worthy prison nicknames would be "Jerry the Affable," "Genial Jake" and "Benny Convicted-of-felony-murder-but-basically-just-a-regular-guy-when-you-get-to-know-him."

Notorious prison rioter and man with a more respectable nickname in prison circles, Sammy "the Bear" (not to be confused with Sammy "the Bull," whose testimony resulted in the jailing of "Teflon Don" John Gotti, so known because "Polytetrafluoroethylene Don" just doesn't have the same ring to it), upon briefly tasting freedom before being sent back to the jug, decided also to taste a few pints and whoop it up at a local pub in Lancashire, much to the shock of the boozy assembly there.

The dancing "Bear," on the very day of his sentencing hearing, downed lagers and boogied around the bar to his favourite songs— what they were was not reported, but pure conjecture on the part of the authors has Tammy Wynette's version of the Elvis hit "Teddy Bear" being a likely candidate. He left the bar, said the source, only when the staff refused to turn up the music.

The 42-year-old boasted he was "going to Barlinnie" (and in anticipation of possible blank stares from readers, let us explain that it is a notorious 19th-century prison on the outskirts of Glasgow).

In court later that day, the inciter of the six-day siege at Peterhead Prison in 1987 and noted Barlinnie alumnus appeared knackered, wavering on his feet as charges were read against him related to an incident that had occurred during a jail transfer. It had taken a gang of 25 prison guards to contain the well-nicknamed Bear during that transfer, after he broke down a door and swung a chunk of wood at prison staff in the manner of Hank Aaron (or his cricketing equivalent).

A court source told the *Sunday Mail* that the Bear said he knew he was going to be sentenced for an additional stint and that he wanted to have a few drinks before he was sent down the river.

Hooch and the Flying Pooch

CORVALLIS GAZETTE TIMES (U.S.), JANUARY 2006;
LINCOLN CITY NEWS GUARD (U.S), JANUARY 2006

Incredibly, the phrase "flying dog" entered into Google generates 330,000 hits—which is somewhat less than astounding when you consider that even plunking "flying alligator" into the search engine generates nearly 2,000.

At this point, if you haven't grown weary of the litter lining the information superhighway and you Google hard enough (clenching your fists might help), you just might come across the tale of an Oregon man who tossed man's best friend out the window of a moving vehicle. Now, as any dog lover knows, in disciplining the beasts this manoeuvre goes above and beyond rubbing little Dagwood's nose in that corner pile of shit.

Ernie, 42, and Millie, 67 (names have been changed), were speeding around late at night in their Ford Bronco (we shall resist, for the sake of this poor beleaguered brand, the temptation to make an O.J. reference) when Ernie reportedly tossed Millie's pet pooch out of the window.

An Oregon State police trooper subsequently stopped to check on a parked vehicle where several people appeared to be looking for something, i.e., the recently launched flea-ridden projectile.

Ernie, who police said was "visibly intoxicated," was waving a knife in Millie's face and for that was taken into custody. While en route to the jail, officers claim, the pooch pitcher attempted to kick out the rear window of the deputy's patrol car. He later assaulted a Lincoln County Jail corrections deputy.

Millie was arrested too, for driving under the influence.

Man's best flying friend was muddied by the landing but, fortunately, sustained only minor abrasions.

IV

Contents May Shift in Transit— Drunk and on the Move

First, let's be clear that the authors of this work in no way condone drinking and driving—that is, unless it is done on a closed course by professionals while filming a car commercial. Drunken go-karting is to be judged by its merits on a case-by-case basis.

No other aspect of public drunkenness gets as much attention as drunk driving, and for good reason—yet no matter how many public service announcements and anti–drunk driving campaigns are run, you know that at the end of the night you may still be holding your third-cousin Dougie in a headlock until he agrees to surrender his car keys and let you call him a cab.

And this is hardly a new development. While we have no historical evidence to back us up, we speculate that as far back as the Bronze Age our antecedents would experience "horse rage," drunkenly plow into one another while giddy on some village fermented rice-and-honey concoction, dismount and knock each other about with whatever tools they had at their disposal, presumably ones made of bronze.

Fast-forward hundreds of years to the time when the first flying machines, ships and automobiles came around and they bestowed on people a sense of wonder, marvel and more importantly freedom—coincidentally characteristics that people have also found at the bottom of a bottle. These developments in transport have increased the number of conveyances that drunks can operate and, as we demonstrate in Contents May Shift in Transit, they are not letting the opportunity go to waste, getting drunk behind the controls of everything from ice-cream trucks to commercial aircraft and all types of nautical vessels.

Drinking has been a part of the seafaring life for hundreds of years, presumably brought on board to help sailors forget about the low pay, dangerous conditions and scurvy. Nowadays, those lolling about in boats in more comfortable conditions continue this seafaring tradition and the word *sailor* almost seems naked without *drunken* preceding it.

Pilots and crew play a relatively small (though admittedly frightening) role in The Mile-High Pie-eyed Club, the focus here being on the passengers they are delivering. These stories show what happens when you stuff an obnoxious drunk into an economy-class seat and provide him with unlimited drinks and an audience for whom escape would mean a drop of several thousand feet.

The drunks here are all in motion. Their destinations may be unclear, but it is certain that rather than escaping their troubles they are on a direct course for more.

11

Chariots of Firewater: Drivers More Gassed Than Their Modes of Transportation

When you drink, don't drive. Don't even putt.

—DEAN MARTIN

Ice-Cream Meltdown

MILWAUKEE JOURNAL SENTINEL, JUNE 2005

One creamy concoction that threatens to leave you with not only a hangover but also the possibility of an ice-cream headache is the delightfully refreshing Kahlua Smoothie. But a 43-year-old ice-cream-truck driver from Milwaukee went right for the hard stuff when he downed the Steel Reserve malt liquor that he was keeping lightly warmed on his dashboard.

All was cool on this speed-limit-abiding drunken joyride until he brazenly tossed an empty into the yard of a self-admitted "freak about littering," who, upon seeing the errant hooch fly, immediately alerted the local constabulary.

This was bad news for the driver, who is a remarkable two for two when it comes to getting fired from ice-cream-truck-driving-related employment due to drinking on the job.

The driver later said that someone had given him the can of beer, and, realizing that it might not reflect on him well as a seller of ice cream to schoolkids if he was seen knocking it back, he poured it out and threw the can on the woman's lawn.

Nonetheless, police arrived and the ice-cream man checked in at three times the legal blood-alcohol level, though in an impassioned defence worthy of Clarence Darrow, he brought into question the very validity of the Breathalyzer test, declaring: "I told [the officer] there was something wrong with that machine. He said there wasn't."

This Little Piggy Should've Stayed Home

Beaver Dam Daily Citizen (U.S.), January 2006;
Wisconsin News, January 2006

If your sensitive stomach can handle the thought of strange fingers rooting around in the candy bowl at the pub, breath mints might seem a great way to hoodwink your roadside interrogator. But rather than masking the odour of the carafe of cheap wine you slugged back at the company picnic, mints are more likely to make your vile breath sugary and do nothing whatsoever for the telltale smell of alcohol emanating from your every pore.

If you do find yourself illuminated in the unholy beam of a patrolman's flashlight it is best to keep the chitchat to a minimum, cross your fingers, uncross your eyes and hope for the best. What won't help you is the presence of a farm animal in your vehicle, or saying, when the subject of sobriety tests is broached: "I'm drunk—

why do them?" as one Wisconsin man did after police arrested him following reports of erratic driving in the area.

When officers approached the vehicle they noticed a man asleep in the driver's seat, and in the back seat, oinking away, a pig—yes, the animal, not a disparaging term for a cop or a lady friend who may not have been at her most presentable.

A strong odour emanated from the vehicle—understandable given the heady bouquet of livestock and grog—and along with the porker, authorities found in the back seat an empty fifth of vodka and an unopened case of beer.

The man, after uttering his notorious words regarding the sobriety tests, was booked on a charge of driving under the influence.

When police asked him why he had behaved so irresponsibly, the man replied that he was angry after a spat with his woman. We can only hope he was not referring to his back-seat passenger.

DISHONOURABLE MENTION
Know Your Giant Monoliths

No matter how lost you are or how many maps you've folded into assorted origami animals, it is never advisable to ask a cop for directions when you're drunk behind the wheel. A 44-year-old New South Wales man might have earned himself a mention in this book solely for having done that; however, he further distinguished himself by removing any and all doubts that the policemen may have been entertaining about his drunken state by asking directions to Uluru, the world's greatest monolith—which was just 109 yards away.

Uluru, or Ayer's Rock, is a massive rock formation that casts a mighty shadow over its flat surroundings at 1,120 feet in height. To circle its base requires a 6-mile drive. Police said that the man's headlights were shining on the rock at the time he asked for directions.

Not surprisingly the man was immediately given a Breathalyzer test, which he of course failed, earning him a charge of drunk driving while unlicensed. (ABC News Online, Australia, March 2006)

The Flat Foot and the Flat Tire

Ananova.com (U.K.), December 2005

Most people's knowledge of jurisprudence comes from reruns of *Baretta, Barney Miller* or the current crop of acronymous crime shows like *SVU* or *CSI.* If there's anything these shows have taught us—besides a smattering of Latin, and how to grab a recalcitrant colleague and/or suspect and hurl him into your locker by the lapels—it's that you always get a chance to make that one call, usually to your lawyer.

In Germany, a drunk driver displayed such foolishness with the telephone prior to his arrest that he deserved to have been denied that one privilege strictly on principle.

Having been sidetracked with a flat tire, the drunk driver decided to phone for help (thus breaking the unwritten male protocol stating that you always change your own tire unless you're a sissy). Much worse for him, however, was that in his compromised state he unknowingly phoned not roadside assistance, but the police emergency line.

Presumably he missed hearing "Hello—Police" on the other end, because the 31-year-old driver blurted out that he had no licence, that he was driving drunk and that the mechanic better arrive post-haste because things could turn ugly for him if the cops were to happen by.

An officer, speaking of the easy arrest in a display of the much-heralded Teutonic wit, quipped: "He wanted us to come quickly, so we did."

DISHONOURABLE MENTION
Getting Plowed

New Yorkers, when bombarded with crappy weather, generally take it in their stride and put on a happy grin. In a February 2006 blizzard, some even cross-country skied along Broadway Avenue.

One snowplow driver in Queens, though, was in too festive a mood during this most recent blast of wintry weather. While clearing the roads of snow, he was completely plowed himself.

Indeed the crippling snowstorm was relatively harmless when compared with the danger posed by the drunk driver. "There's a big yellow plow coming towards me, why isn't he stopping?" noted a frantic witness, who called police from a cell phone from his vehicle.

The witness said that the driver was red-faced, had his shirt open and that his chest looked red—these being indicators of either some kind of bizarre torso-slapping contest or, as the witness ventured, "the basic signs of someone being drunk."

The driver crashed his rig into two cars before being pulled out of the plow. The 60-year-old driver declined a Breathalyzer test and was charged with driving under the influence.

Residents of Queens feeling antsy about the next heavy snowfall may rest assured that the offending driver was suspended from the sanitation department. (WABC TV, U.S., February 2006)

Not So Happy Meal

BRIDGETON NEWS, FEBRUARY 2006; NJ.COM, FEBRUARY 2006; CNN, FEBRUARY 2006

In Las Vegas you can tie the knot without the hassle of even leaving your car. Yes, Sin City offers drive-through weddings, which just adds to the myriad services offered at the drive-through, including pet grooming, prayer drop-offs, lottery tickets, flu shots and, for the tug at the old heartstrings (or at the very least the purse strings), marriage vow renewals.

In most other parts of the country, though, the best you can hope for after the drive-through is that the spouse you already have won't mind your breath or the gas that results from the greasy bag of food you order from the surly-sounding woman on the drive-through's speaker.

A Bridgeton, New Jersey, man was arrested after throwing a fit at the drive-through window of one particular fast-food joint. Upon receiving his meal, the would-be gastronome inspected his patties (good move) and found meat in there that was pinker than the wardrobe of a pair of twin 6-year-old girls.

The man's remonstrations after having received burgers that were still on the grazing side of medium rare were such that the police had to be called. When they arrived they found the man three sheets to the wind and pacing back and forth in a state of great agitation. He demanded that the police summon the local Action News team for an on-the-spot exposé of the underdone beef being dished out by the establishment.

Perhaps sensing that local news sources would be hesitant to rush to the location to chase down a scoop from an aspiring Barbara Walters with booze breath, they told him to get lost, at which point he cussed out the patrolmen, telling them to go ahead, beat him up and take him to jail.

He was arrested for disorderly conduct and issued a summons for being smashed in public; however, the budding restaurant critic clearly was not considered a hardened criminal, because he was later driven home by police.

DISHONOURABLE MENTION
To the Chagrin of the Bare Skin Finn

In Oslo, a man was arrested on a bus while completely stewed and naked, thus setting a record with an estimated 99 unpaid fines for disorderly conduct. The man is known for off-the-cuff burlesque routines, shedding pieces of clothing with increasing levels of inebriation.

The fatuous Finn, who goes by multiple identities, has been repeatedly expelled from Norway, but, like a case of athlete's foot, keeps returning. (Associated Press, December 2005; *The Local*, Sweden, December 2005)

From Backyard to Prison Yard

BC Cycle, November 2005; The Associated Press, November 2005

Hustler—the company that makes lawnmowers, not the magazine known for having more beaver shots than Canadian tourism literature—claims that its Super Z riding mower is the "fastest of the fast." While this may be likened to being the healthiest thing on the menu at Big Al's House of Miscellaneous Meat, the bearcat can certainly burn rubber, or at least the back-forty equivalent, at 24 to 28 horses and a top speed of 15 miles per hour. With Kawasaki thrust, this liquid-cooled bad boy can leave covetous cousin Randal and his antiquated push-mower in the dust (provided there is a mighty wind kicking up)—although on the downside, it also guzzles more gas than a Hummer in rush hour.

Riding mowers are getting faster, but manufacturers may want to think twice before making cup holders standard, following the drunken antics of one helmsman in a Springfield, Illinois, cornfield.

A radio call told police to be on the lookout for a man absconding with a stolen vehicle—the vehicle in question being a hot riding mower.

An officer driving in a rural part of town spotted the man almost as soon as the description "bouncing through the cornfield with his ponytail flopping in the breeze" went out. Ruling out the possibility of coincidence, the officer phoned in sheriff's deputies, who formed a perimeter around the suspect and demanded that he get off the mower.

Surrounded and apparently oblivious to what mode of transportation he was on—a Super Z it was not—the suspect balked and slowly trundled farther down the field. Baffled by the man's bluster, given his snail-like mode of transportation and the fact that all the policemen were in cars, a sheriff's deputy nonetheless exited his vehicle and began to jog alongside the man.

This chase scene, which Steve McQueen would've brought to the big screen had he lived to be 110 years old, drew to a close when, tired of the jog, officers threatened to zap the 45-year-old joyrider with a stun-gun.

It turned out the inebriated fellow was on parole at the time, and as a result of his antics he faced a return trip to the slammer.

Ripped Runaway Researcher

SKY NEWS (ITALY), SEPTEMBER 2003; SMOKINGGUN.COM, SEPTEMBER 2003

Germany and Italy take their speeding laws seriously, and unlike, say, the super-charged Chevy Impala cop car over here, which can be left in the dust by a 17-year-old kid with a modified import, a heavy foot and tacky neon under-lights, Euro-cops are taking tech steroids in hopes of out-muscling the muscle cars.

In Calabria, Italy, for example, some Italian state troopers have been outfitted with the Lamborghini Gallardo, which takes off at a whiplash-inducing speed of 0-to-60 mph in four seconds, enough to test the warranty on any pacemaker as well as leave an improperly affixed hairpiece in the rear seat—if the vehicle had one. Not to be outdone, German Polizei lead-foots can burn rubber in Porsche 911s equipped to handle speeds of more than 182 miles per hour to nail culprits in the Autobahn's "slow lane."

Police in Pennsylvania, underpowered as they may have been in comparison with their European counterparts, still managed to catch up with a runaway research chemist (with this the first known usage of that phrase in the English language) driving drunk and trying to outrun them at speeds of 182 mph in a Lamborghini Diablo.

The ripped egghead, who used an important family occasion that he needed to attend as the excuse for his G-Force–like speed on the road, undoubtedly would have left cops eating dirt like that corrupt mayor in *Dukes of Hazzard* had his luxurious auto not gotten stuck in traffic.

Ordered to exit the high-end piece of Italian engineering, he at first refused. Finally he relented, and "stumbled out of the vehicle" reeking of the hooch.

Four-Wheel Driving Drunk

WFTV FLORIDA, JANUARY 2004

Driving around the back roads in your favourite pickup truck with a topless woman in the front seat ranks quite high in the ultimate male fantasy department, though the fantasy came to a jarring halt in the case of one drunk.

A Florida man, out for a ride in his Chevy, bare-breasted babe at his side and with more than a few beers down his gullet, lost control of his vehicle and sent it careening into a suburban home—carving a hole in one end of the house and exiting the other. The two-ton pickup entered through the house's living room and came to a final stop in the family's backyard pool.

Hearing the thundering crash, the owner of the house thought that an airplane had dropped from the sky. He said that 30 minutes prior to the Chevy passing through he and his family had been watching television, but as providence would have it, they had gone to bed early—their lives thus saved by a weak winter TV lineup.

A neighbour, seeing a geyser of water shooting up from where the crash-in couple had taken out a kitchen sink, was the first to attend to the couple in the Chevy. Although the passenger was half-naked and incoherent and the driver stank of rotgut, both were lucky to survive.

Front-end Loaded

THE GUARDIAN (U.K.), NOVEMBER 2005

The *French Connection* chase scene through the streets of Brooklyn was so riveting that it not only jump-started Gene Hackman's career but made him prematurely bald. The flick also launched the cliché of the renegade cop who'd lost patrol car privileges and was making do with a bus pass, yet always somehow managed to commandeer a civilian's car to nab that bad guy (and the poor sap obligingly handed it over too, despite its predictable wreckage at a grocery stand—and the guy was never compensated either … but we digress).

In southwest England, a chase scene straight out of a bad action flick airing on a Saturday afternoon as a lead-in to *Coronation Street* reruns took place through the delightful countryside, complete with six squad cars and a helicopter in hot—well, lukewarm at least—pursuit.

The pursued in this case was not a cop killer, baby snatcher or swarthy international drug trafficker with a difficult-to-place accent looking to elude police, but a soused teenager driving farm equipment.

The vehicle, a tractor hauling cows and chauffeured by a shellacked farm labourer, took off at an adrenalin-curtailing 10 miles per hour and was spotted swerving across two lanes without lights. It led cops on a low-speed pursuit for nearly an hour, as the driver swung his trailer out on the road to cut off the gendarmes every time they came close.

At one point, the farm hand tried to ram a police car by reversing the tractor into it, a move that might have proved successful had he not been pulling a livestock trailer, which jackknifed—very probably upsetting each of the four stomachs of the traumatized livestock cargo. The driver, who later claimed to have no memory of the chase, was still able to plow forward and might have continued his wild ride for hours if police had not decided to lay stingers, spiked devices used to bring vehicles to a complete stop.

DISHONOURABLE MENTION
Drunk at the Reins

In England, a fruit-and-vegetable trader gave police a run for their money on his brown-and-white mare. The 40-year-old was chased a mile and a half by two cops in a cruiser, whose attempted interception at one point consisted of their jumping out of their car, standing in the middle of the road and frantically waving their arms at him.

Just like in the cartoons, however, they had to dive out of the way as the hosed horseman bore down on them.

The man pleaded guilty to being drunk while in charge of a horse and carriage, likely the last time ever that that charge will be brought up in these industrialized times. (*The Guardian*, U.K., July 1984)

Off the Rails

New York Times, November 1982

Train engineers always have a story to tell. Whether it involves playing chicken with that rusted-out Oldsmobile at the railway crossing or trying to stop a tremendously high mass with relatively low braking friction as it careens into a passing buffalo stampede, the job presents constant challenges.

Who among us as youngsters (at least, the ones not interested in becoming firemen, cops, astronauts, athletes, doctors, nurses, actors, et cetera) didn't entertain the prospect of donning the blue overalls, striped hat and effete red bandana of a train conductor? These jauntily attired gents, as we kids knew, are entrusted to haul shipments of dangerous and explosive chemicals and other hazardous cargo such as radioactive waste all over the continent.

It seems the 101-car freight train wasn't the only thing loaded with toxic materials when it jumped its rails in Louisiana: the engineer was sleeping off the effects of his drinking.

A court later heard that the conductor was in such bad shape he could no longer sit upright. In his place as he dozed was a young railroad clerk who had the dubious credentials of having "some knowledge of how it was done," having tested out locomotives in the yard.

In the ensuing investigation into the railroad debacle, which forced the evacuation of nearly 3,000 residents, the clerk in question was asked why she didn't take measures to stop the train once she saw that her boss was incapacitated. The clerk told investigators she was fearful that they would lose their jobs and hoped that her boss would eventually come around and take control of the train again.

Clearly the clerk had vastly overestimated the recuperative powers of the conductor. Not only did he fail to rouse himself to prevent the train's derailment, but he was also noticeably absent when it was his turn to testify at a hearing looking into his misconduct.

Hot Under the Collar

AGENCE FRANCE-PRESSE (FRANCE), NOVEMBER 2004;

ANANOVA.COM (U.K.), NOVEMBER 2004

The first miracle in the Christian tradition—and probably the one most celebrated by believers and secularists alike—is believed to have occurred when Jesus changed water into wine at a wedding that was running out of the stuff in Cana town.

An excerpt from John 2.9–10 reads: "When the ruler of the feast had tasted the water that was made wine, and knew not whence it was, the governor of the feast called the bridegroom, / And saith unto him, Every man at the beginning doth set forth good wine; and when men have well drunk, then that which is worse: but thou hast kept the good wine until now."

According to our resident biblical scholar, this can be interpreted as: It is customary for hosts to serve their best wine first, and later, when partiers are smashed and their taste buds beaten into submission, to bring out the plonk. You, good sir, have kept the primo stuff out for the entire shout. Well done.

A Croatian priest charged with several criminal offences in one day could have done with some divine intervention and a reversing of this miracle.

The priest, who later defended himself by saying that even the Pope makes mistakes, got into a heated argument with a parishioner after allegedly consuming more than the prescribed amount of sacramental wine. The priest punched the congregant in the face and cut his eye.

The padre, known as "The Sheriff"—an alarming nickname for a man of the cloth—then threatened others with a rifle before taking off in his car, and ended the night by crashing into a tree. When police finally caught up with this particularly vibrant vicar, he refused to submit to a Breathalyzer test.

The town bishop defended the priest by saying that he did not act alone—that "the wine was with him."

Divine DUI Exemption

Priests in Croatia, an overwhelmingly Catholic country, sought to be exempted from a zero-tolerance drunk-driving law passed in 2004, citing the excuse that priests often have to drink wine as many as three times a day as a part of mass. (BBC, July 2004)

The Blind Leading the Blind (Drunk)

UNITED PRESS INTERNATIONAL (U.S.), MAY 1985

Designated drivers are the martyrs of the beer-nut set. While everyone else around them is getting wildly debauched and increasingly obnoxious, the designated driver remains sober, suffering the lot of them and forced to stay to the bitter end to see everyone home safely. It's the sort of duty you get stuck with after losing a bet, or while on parole.

For a designated-driver program to work, however, you must first be sure that the people entrusted with this duty are reliable—that they are not taking clandestine pulls from a concealed flask; that they have valid driver's licences; and, most importantly, that they are able to distinguish objects and light.

A Virginia couple capped off a night of drinking at a tavern at about 3 A.M. The female half of that couple, 20, had driven to the bar but felt too drunk to make the return trip. It was decided that her male companion, 24, should take over at the wheel, as he was the less drunk of the two. But what puts this past the point of muddled logic is that the man in question was blind.

The blind man, who was being given directions by his sozzled partner in crime, was, not surprisingly, a very bad driver. A police officer spotted the car weaving dangerously across three lanes of traffic and followed it for a few miles before signalling for it to pull over.

Once he had ordered the driver out of the vehicle, the officer noticed that the man seemed to have no control over his eyes, even less so than the other glassy-eyed barflies he was accustomed to pulling over at that time of night. After some questioning, the driver explained that he was blind—a driving handicap topped off by the fact he was roaring drunk to the point of slurring his speech and needing to lean against the vehicle to support himself.

The blind driver was given a suspended sentence, but warned that if he ever got behind the wheel of a car again he would be sent to jail.

DISHONOURABLE MENTION
Spinning Your Wheels

Although carney folk might not be counted on to properly bolt down the Vomit Comet Roller Coaster every time, circuses remain a living, breathing link to the spectacles of ancient Rome.

An Ohio man was taken into custody for operating a Ferris wheel well into his cups. Bond was set at $1,000, the monetary equivalent of 350 stuffed toy elephants won in the ring toss. The careless carney was charged with one count of endangering kids, who were on the ride at the time, after he was asked to "Step right up, don't be shy" to the Breathalyzer machine. (WKYC TV; WCPO TV Ohio; Channel 5 Cincinnati, July 2005)

12

Mile-High Pie-Eyed Club: High Altitudes, Unlimited Booze and the Fun That Follows

You define a good flight by negatives: you didn't get hijacked, you didn't crash, you didn't throw up, you weren't late, you weren't nauseated by the food. So you're grateful.

—PAUL THEROUX

Ripped Robinson Crusoe

CBC NEWS, DECEMBER 2005; *THE TIMES OF LONDON,* DECEMBER 2005

It's been said that "no man is an island," but this assertion was put to the test on a flight from England to Spain when a passenger more marinated than Greek calamari was dumped off on his own little patch of land.

After a foul-mouthed tirade against the flight crew—which if we were to reproduce it here would contain many asterisks, exclamation points and assorted glyphs—the passenger was exiled like Napoleon on the tiny island of Porto Santo off the North African coast, and was sued by the airline for the cost of the unscheduled diversion.

The passenger was kicked off the plane, and his luggage dumped from the hold, before the jet carrying 200 other passengers took off again, leaving him to ponder his fate.

Porto Santo's claim to fame as a desert island is the stuff of legend because of its near-complete absence of vegetation, putting it far down on the list of deserted islands on which you would like to be stranded.

It's unclear how or when the crocked commuter would return to Britain after the incident, Porto Santo being a two-and-a-half-hour ferry ride to the nearest airport. An airline spokesperson said that the man would most definitely not be making the journey on one of their flights.

(Play) Mating Rituals: Playmates Arrested

CBS4 COLORADO, DECEMBER 2005; SMOKINGGUN.COM, DECEMBER 2005

Playboy playmates are known to guzzle high-end scotch and raw oysters with abandon while re-enacting slice-of-life pieces from the heyday of Sodom and Gomorrah in Hef's infamous grotto—or so the stories go. And then there are the tickle fights … That said, playmates can be forgiven for operating by an entirely different social code from the rest of us.

Two bodacious babes, whose bounties were laid bare for all to see as *Playboy*'s "Cybergirls of the Month," were arrested after a drunken mid-air incident that would have had Bob Guccione calling for backup (and another vodka and Clamato).

Police allege that while in the air the pair became so exceedingly stinko that they started a tussle with one another, and other passengers

and police deemed them to be "a danger to themselves and others."
Now it's very possible they were a danger to themselves, but rushing
gallantly to their defence we must add that it is very unlikely they were
a danger to others. That is, unless by "danger" they were referring to
the playmates' making sexually suggestive comments, shedding articles
of clothing and behaving in a lewd and lascivious manner.

Anyway, we'll leave this in the realm of your imagination and
continue with the facts.

The women did not take kindly to being arrested for public
intoxication upon landing at San Antonio International Airport.
They were "cussing," according to a police report, and telling anyone
who would listen that they were celebrities—in the best Warhol sense
of that term—and that police had "fucked" with the wrong people.

The arresting officer's report also alleges that one of the women
made a sexual advance toward both the primary officer and the
backup. To their credit—and remarkably, given the dearth of
Playboy models making such offers on a policeman's average day—
both officers refused her favours.

Cabin Pressure: The Crew Goes Wild

BBC News, July 2004; MosNews.com (Russia), July 2004

When we fly, we like to make ourselves at home, tiny and cramped
as the space may be. To pass the time, some passengers favour the
assembled with percussive samba beats knocked out on the food tray
while consuming as many gin and tonics as can be surreptitiously
nicked from the service cart. Overtaken by an ambrosial glow,
others take great delight in the playful pinching of flight attendants'

bottoms, not exactly endearing themselves to the service-people of the sky. Some even coarser seatmates engage in less whimsical behaviours, occasionally driving flight attendants to the brink.

Perhaps succumbing to this type of cabin pressure, attendants on a Russian flight turned the tables on passengers by commandeering the drinks cart themselves, proceeding to get gonzo and unleashing their own mile-high hijinks.

Passengers on a flight from Moscow to a small city in Siberia, who already had to face the bleak prospect of reaching their far from Club Med–like destination, were deprived of their in-flight meal, and two were even physically attacked by attendants drunker than the first three rows of a tough-man contest.

Passengers had to interrupt the crew's soiree to demand their in-flight meals, which had yet to be served, and the attendants grudgingly complied—just as the plane was making its final descent. Suffice to say, this is not the optimal time to have dinner served, as meals (the half that did arrive) ended up mostly on the floor and in travellers' laps.

One particularly demanding passenger had the audacity to request to be served by a sober and competent attendant. Attendants proceeded to administer a sound beating to him for his troubles, which required him to seek medical attention upon landing.

The Mother Loaded

TORONTO STAR, DECEMBER 1995; REUTERS, DECEMBER 1995

In psychiatric circles (which we travel in every now and then to get prescriptions renewed), the "locus of control" is a theoretical construct that examines a person's perceived control over his or her behaviour. An "external" locus indicates that one perceives others to have control over events in one's life—like the head of the Freemasons who's giving directives to that guy at the bus terminal. An "internal" locus means that the individual believes that his/her behaviour is guided by personal decisions and efforts.

In the following tale, a mother and daughter demonstrated that they could've used a steaming heap of the latter when they blamed the airline for their own outrageous behaviour and that of 16 other passengers who started a near riot in mid-air.

The group of British and Irish tourists kept the wheels on the complimentary drinks trolley in motion for most of the flight, getting completely mangled and becoming so unruly that one of them was later held on charges of assault and intimidating a crew member. Other members of the ugly 18 were corralled by U.S. Olympic wrestlers, whose fortuitous presence on the flight was undoubtedly a welcome relief to beleaguered flight attendants.

The mother and daughter combo, chosen by the media to be the spokespeople of this disruptive lot, laid the blame squarely on the airline. "They gave us drinks on the plane and shouldn't have," said the mother, to which her daughter, in a case of the fermented apple not falling too far from the tree, added: "Why were they giving out drinks?"

Airline staff members and other passengers were probably asking themselves the same question, as the pilot was forced to make an unscheduled landing so that the blasted tourists could be shown the door—unfortunately not 20,000 feet in the air at the time.

The Nude Avenger

COURIER-MAIL (AUSTRALIA), OCTOBER 1985

The cardigan sweater was named after the seventh Earl of Cardigan, James Thomas Brudenell, who was likely laughed at by Russian gunners as they mowed down his troops in the charge of the Light Brigade during the Crimean War. The avuncular button-up accoutrement that bears his name was popularized in the modern day by Jimmy Carter and Mr. Rogers and has come to be associated with slow, soothing talkers. But the duds may never be looked upon the same way again by travellers on a flight en route to Singapore.

Accepted seat-belt protocol was violated as a Melbourne man and British citizen, 47, got out of his seat when the seat-belt sign was clearly on—but only after stripping down to only a cardigan worn back to front. Officials say the violently drunk, nude-from-the-waist-down man paraded through the cabin upsetting the complimentary peanuts of more than one of his fellow passengers.

It took seven crew members to subdue the man, who was turning the high-pressured air blue with his decidedly non-PG language and attempting to open the doors of the aircraft. "I'm getting off the bus," the confused man cried.

The incident was later dubbed "disgraceful" by an international cabin crew association spokesman. The drunken man in question was detained in Singapore before being peppered with questions by his police escort on the flight back.

The High-Flying Maltese Falcons

BBC News, November 1998

Some say the fear of flying isn't really about the risks and inherent dangers, but, much like punching a time card down at the nail-gun testing centre, it has more to do with the discomforting awareness that your life is not under your control.

Once you've strapped yourself in, shoved that suitcase bursting with contraband under your seat, anxiously closed your eyes during the demo of what to do if cabin pressure is ever lost and called out for that double gin and tonic before the plane has even left the tarmac, you've got yourself into a fine existentialist mess there, mister. People deal with this perceived loss of control in different ways. Some breathe more heavily than a peep show regular, while others toast the Wright Brothers' invention and drink themselves into another stratosphere.

On a flight from Birmingham to Malta, shortly after takeoff a father and son proceeded to knock back whisky and beer, getting themselves more ripped than a Mr. Universe finalist.

The dad, a 61-year-old Maltese national, got pickled on the Boeing 757 flight because he was petrified of flying, the court heard later. But it was an act of unrequited love that forced the plane to be diverted to Milan. The senior gentleman told flight attendants, "I want to see the captain, I love him!" The captain, not sharing these feelings of adulation, kept himself locked in the cockpit.

One terrified female passenger was trapped in the lavatory as the father and son brawled with other passengers in the aisle, head-butting one, who later required hospitalization.

The man and his 27-year-old son were jailed for 12 months for their part in the fracas.

Raging Granny at 20,000 Feet

The Independent (U.K.), April 2000; Salon.com (U.S.), April 2000

The stereotypical granny is one who always has a ready supply of hard candy and knits cozies for various small electrical appliances. What one typically does not think of when one hearkens back to times spent at the surgical-stocking-clad knee of dear old Grandma is a rum-drunk woman letting forth a stream of curses that would have had even your most hardened insult-comic calling for earplugs.

A 56-year-old grandmother of 10 (editor's note: wow) got so drunk, vocal and physical on a flight from Manchester, England, to Florida that her actions got her jailed for six months.

Matters started off quietly enough. As far as airport staff knew, the woman drank three Bacardi and Cokes and when they noticed that she was getting "somewhat merry," they cut her off. Unbeknownst to them, however, the woman also had a bottle of duty-free rum under her seat, which was later found—amazingly, given the woman's age and the relatively short flight time between England and Florida—three-quarters empty.

As the flight progressed and the bottle of Bacardi emptied, she became increasingly loud and repeatedly called air attendants to complain about the food, all the while using words in front of children that they certainly wouldn't hear outside of school, popular music or cable television.

As the plane came in for landing the granny stood up, and when a flight attendant asked her to sit down, she slugged the crew member three times on the side of the face. Granny continued to carry on and kick as she was pulled off the plane in Florida. Air crew had to take her out in a wheelchair, presumably Hannibal Lecter style, to get her off the plane.

The granny later said that she remembered the gentleman sitting next to her on the plane buying her three drinks—and nothing else until she woke up on the floor of the U.S. immigration office.

Flying the Very Friendly Skies

TELEGRAPH (AUSTRALIA), SEPTEMBER 1985;
AUSTRALIAN ASSOCIATED PRESS, SEPTEMBER 1985

On first-class flights, or so we've been told, flight attendants dangle cherries above eagerly salivating gums, massage bunions, give back rubs and ply passengers with champagne—the kind from north-eastern France, not the cheap stuff that goes by the same signature but comes in a crate.

A passenger on a flight to Hawaii told a court in Auckland that he had had sex with an off-duty flight attendant in the plane's rest room. He and his new-found paramour then toasted one another with champagne, in economy class.

The flight attendant, perhaps light-headed after the lavatory lovin' and the downing of five glasses of the good stuff, fell over, and, according to a flight purser, London, France and the woman's underpants were not visible at the time.

The hostess with the mostest was assisted to the front of the plane by two members of the cabin crew, after which the passenger returned to his seat and, ever the romantic, fell asleep.

The purser helped the woman to her seat, but a few minutes later she was "climbing onto a passenger," a fellow off-duty crew member who was sitting with his wife. The attendant, who later sought reinstatement and recompense from the airline, sat on the passenger's armrest with her legs wrapped around the passenger's neck, the court heard.

Defence counsel submitted that sleeping tablets and alcohol had combined to create the incident, which the flight attendant later could not seem to remember.

Pop!

The longest champagne-cork flight in recorded history was 177 feet and 9 inches—4 feet from ground level at Woodbury Vineyards in New York. (Dipsomania.com)

Ground Control to Major Bombed

CALGARY HERALD, MARCH 1990

If you have a fear of flying—that is, if you're the type that ignores the emergence of discount airlines and continues to take long-haul buses and trains and would opt to hitchhike with a psychopath trucker rather than get on a plane—you might want to skip this story entirely. On the other hand, if you're looking for something to strengthen and legitimize your fears, you would do well to make photocopies of this to hand out to those who scoff at your aversion to flight.

A pilot and two of his officers were scheduled to take off on a pre-dawn flight from Fargo, North Dakota, to Minneapolis, Minnesota, and booked a room at a local hotel, ostensibly to get some shut-eye beforehand. Of course, if they had done that they wouldn't have found their way into the pages of this book.

Instead, the trio decided to look for a little action in the surrounding area at about 5:30 P.M. They found it at a local bar and restaurant that was right in the midst of celebrating "Bang-Bang Hour" on "Whoopee Wednesday." The three fly boys had their share of both bang-bang and whoopee, drinking excessively for the next five hours. Investigators later discovered from receipts that the pilot, the leader of the group and therefore the one obligated to out-drink his inferiors, had set the pace with 15 or more rum and Cokes. His two co-pilots had left the bar shortly before him, but still managed to put down six pitchers of beer between them.

The three eventually made their way back to the hotel late that night, and the next morning at 5:15 A.M. were driven to the airport. Unbeknownst to them, someone from the bar had overheard what the pilots did for a living when they got into a drunken argument with another bar patron, and had phoned airline officials to let them know that the trio were unfit to fly.

They were met at the airport by an inspector who was unsure how to proceed, later saying that the three had not been visibly intoxicated. While he was on the phone with relevant officials, he witnessed the Boeing 727 taking off.

The flight, which transported 91 passengers to Minneapolis where they had to land during a violent ice storm, reached its desti-nation safely, but on the ground the pilots were met by a Federal

Aviation Administration (FAA) inspector who put them under citizen's arrest. Police then took blood samples from the three men. Both co-pilots clocked in at over the FAA's .04-percent blood-alcohol limit, and the pilot showed why he was the boss by coming in at an astonishing .12 percent, well over the legal limit and the point at which experts say that motor reflexes are dulled and judgment is seriously impaired. It was estimated that he would have registered .24 percent when he left the bar the previous night—a level at which most people would be unable to walk.

All three pilots were fired over the incident, and the offending airline issued an apology to customers, many of whom in future are more likely to be found next to you on a Greyhound bus trip than in the friendly skies.

On a Wing and a Prayer

WNBC TV Channel 4 NYC, June 2005; *Danbury News Times*, June 2006

Driving a car is fairly basic. In fact, a variety-show-trained dancing simian (or any comparable creature with a prehensile thumb) could likely master the task, at least when driving an automatic.

While in most jurisdictions the ability to recognize a stop sign in a written test will result in the granting of at least a temporary driver's licence, the Federal Aviation Administration is much more thorough, mandating a minimum of 20 flight hours to obtain a sport pilot certificate.

A wasted 20-year-old Connecticut man didn't let his mere seven hours of training, lack of a pilot's licence, a blood alcohol level nearly double that of the state's legal limit for driving a car or the fact that two minors were present dissuade him from chauffeuring his two friends around on a nearly four-hour joyride, which came to an inauspicious end when he got lost, began to run out of fuel and was forced to land.

When security met up with the waste-bag fly boy, which occurred with haste as the airport at which he landed had been closed for five hours, a "significant number of beer cans" fell out the cockpit door.

The wannabe pilot accepted a plea deal in Superior Court that would sentence him to a one-year term in the slammer, as the judge, invoking the post–9/11 paranoia of our times, noted that he risked being shot out of the sky as a suspected terrorist, and didn't do himself any favours by kicking at security guards who tried to apprehend him.

13
Sloshed at Sea: What Shall We Do with a Drunken Sailor?

If one does not know to which port one is sailing,
no wind is favourable.

—Seneca

Row, Row, Row Your Hooch

Agence France-Presse, May 1995

When most of us think of having to go that extra distance to secure our next drink, it's along the lines of bypassing that neglectful eye-contact-avoiding waitress and approaching the bar ourselves. Rarely, unless we're in a bad part of a town or at a rodeo, would we actually risk personal injury for a libation. However, if the desire is strong enough, the lengths a person will go to for their favourite tipple can take on mother-lifting-vehicle-to-free-trapped-infant–like proportions.

A Russian sailor working on a dry trawler 3 miles from the coast of New Zealand had such a powerful hankering for some vodka that he commandeered a child's dinghy and paddled himself to shore to procure it.

The sailor set out in the blow-up dinghy just 5 feet in length, with plastic paddles and its bargain-basement price of $55 written on the side in black felt pen.

He made it to land, purchased eight bottles of vodka, sampled enough of it to get drunk and four hours later set out to bring his cache of booze back to the trawler. Meanwhile the weather at sea had worsened and the sailor soon found himself struggling against heavy winds in a flimsy vessel better suited to a large backyard pool than to choppy seas.

Fortunately for the sailor, a port watchman spotted the dinghy floundering in the water and police were called in to assist him. The drunken sailor was rescued and arrested. He claimed that he wasn't scared of the sea because he had a life jacket—a jacket the arresting officer described as "something out of a World War II submarine—it was rotten and had holes in it."

Police called the sailor's ship by radio and were told plainly by the captain that they could keep the sailor as long as they pleased.

The next day, however, police returned the sailor to his ship with the vodka in tow.

Better Dinghies Cost More

A Plastimo model inflatable dinghy with oar-locks, stoppers, aluminum-reinforced pads and maximum abrasion resistance, a repair kit and a bellows pump retails for US$1,093.39, though much crappier models, such as the one featured in this story, can and do sell for much less. (Marine.com)

That Sinking Feeling

PRESS ASSOCIATION (U.K.), SEPTEMBER 2005;

ANANOVA.COM (U.K.), SEPTEMBER 2005

Most married men have someplace they can repair to when things with the missus are heading for a night spent on the lumpy old couch that smells of Doritos and your cousin Billy the moocher who just shipped out last week. Places like the corner bar provide men with sanctuaries where they can dodge the shrill screams of home, commiserate with other poor slobs and receive terrible pieces of advice on how to smooth things over with the other half. But others seek more innovative escapes.

A drunken 52-year-old Dutch man living in Southampton, England, was looking to put some distance between him and his wife after an argument and, rather than seeking out the local bar, he decided to take a cache of beer and set out to sea on his untested and half-completed power boat.

The boat had been an ongoing project of his for three years—the type of project that every man who has lived at the same address for long enough is bound to attempt, and ultimately to leave unfinished for his heirs to dispose of and the termites to devour.

The powerboat had all the correct equipment in place, but none of the electronics worked and the man was unable to operate the engine. By the time the sailor was spotted and towed back by a yacht in Weymouth Bay, he had been drifting at sea for two days with nothing on board but the beer he had brought to drink after his marital spat.

The official said the man was lucky that the weather hadn't been worse, because the boat was unsound. There were no portholes on the vessel—just empty spaces where the glass should have been.

Upon being returned to dry land, the drunken sailor was given a stern lecture, but officials were skeptical as to how effective it had been. When it was over, the man headed straight for the pub.

Venetian Blind Drunk

ANANOVA.COM (U.K.), FEBRUARY 2004;

AGENZIA GIORNALISTICA ITALIA, FEBRUARY 2004

The threat of terrorism, so we're told, is such that it could conceivably be anywhere we look and take any form. Ever notice how that man selling ice cream on a cart attached to a bicycle is always smiling on hot days? What exactly is there to be so happy about? Does he *know* something?

Italian police thought a terrorist was what they had on their hands when they received reports that somebody had stolen a waterbus—a large boat used in Venice for quick public transportation around the canals—and was using it to speed recklessly through the canals of Venice, knocking gondolas out of its way and sending them crashing into their moorings, prompting more than one gondolier, we'd wager, to let out a *"Va' fa' un culo"* at the passing vessel. The waterbus was attempting the kind of death-defying turns last seen in *Speed II*.

The chase intensified once police realized that the waterbus was headed directly for a large petrochemical complex. In an effort to stop it, police drew alongside, but the waterbus changed directions and attempted to ram them.

Eventually they were able to stop and board the boat, on which they found not an international terrorist, but a plastered 36-year-old Russian who had stolen the waterbus for a joyride.

The Russian was held on charges of stealing the boat, breaching several navigation rules and resisting arrest.

DISHONOURABLE MENTION
Thar He Blows ... Over

The owners of the *Exxon Valdez,* in an attempt to jettison the cargo-load of bad mojo that resulted from its having spilled millions of gallons of crude oil into the Gulf of Alaska, promptly renamed the ill-fated vessel the *Sea River Mediterranean* for continued operation, though with less than enthusiastic fanfare (no dancing girls) and no champagne broadsides from ribbon-cutters.

In the seafaring tradition of the *Exxon Valdez,* the more-than-5,000-ton Swiss-registered *Kathrin* was run aground by its captain, reflecting the old adage "red eyes in the morning, sailors take warning." The wrecked skip, despite his 30 years of experience on the high seas, was found "drunk and incapable" and slumped over the ship's controls at 8 A.M., his blood-alcohol level four times over the acceptable limit. He was sentenced to seven months in the hoosegow. (*Yorkshire Post Today,* March 2006)

A Seafaring Slice of Life

ASSOCIATED PRESS, NOVEMBER 2005; IMDB.COM, NOVEMBER 2005

The suburban, acne-addled youth meandering into a mall, skateboard under arm and asking for "something Celtic, dude," has chipped away at the sanctity and ritual associated with body art, as has the sad sack who tattoos "Lorna" on his chest, only to be dumped shortly thereafter and doomed the rest of his days to finding a comparably named amour.

Captain Cook and his crew are said to have returned from Polynesian voyages in the 18th century not only with bad cases of crotch rot but also festooned with tattoos, and to this day sailors ritualistically tattoo themselves—especially when first crossing the equator. We assume there is a comparable tradition for sailors who already reside in equatorial countries, for whom such a voyage could be accomplished simply by getting up in the morning.

Bizarre, secretive rituals are part and parcel of seafaring and of many tight-knit groups, but short of being shanghaied or attending a Freemason luau, most of us "civilian" folk are kept out of the loop.

One such bizarre ceremony that occurred aboard a British navy ship involved the drunken crew invoking the name of a made-up sea god, inspired by, of all things, the movie villain in *Ghostbusters*.

Amid chants of "Gozar Gozar," footwear was drunkenly set ablaze in the mess hall with lighter fluid and subsequently doused in the sink. In some instances, as the curious name was chanted and much beer consumed, an unlucky sailor would be pinned down on a table and his shirt ripped open with a knife, which was then pulled back and forth across his stomach until it drew blood.

Thereafter, others volunteered themselves for mutilation out of perceived obligation. "Gozar," incidentally, is also the infinitive form of the Spanish verb meaning "to enjoy," adding an extra helping of irony to the proceedings.

One deserter mechanic was sentenced to 12 months in detention for the serious offence of setting fire aboard a warship, as well as assault and being drunk on board. The volunteers were absolved, presumably because the judge took pity on them for the less-than-enviable part they played in the episode.

Yo-Ho-Ho and a Bottle of Rum

Marco Polo recorded a 14th-century account of a "very good wine of sugar" (rum) that was offered to him in what is modern-day Iran. (Answers.com)

Bathtub S.O.S.

THE HERALD (U.K.), JANUARY 2000; REUTERS, JANUARY 2000

Lit up like the winner's board at a bingo parlour on Saturday night, and playing with his toy ships while taking a bath, a 52-year-old—yes, that's right—Danish man broke from his frivolity to place a call to Denmark's Sea Rescue Command unit.

While the man was (not surprisingly) alone in the tub at the time of his SOS, our sources suggest the call sounded something like this: "I'm the captain of a 12-man freighter and we're going down fast. The situation is dire. The vessel is tilting at a 45-degree angle and already one member of the crew has been washed overboard. Send assistance immediately to prevent any further members of my gallant crew from meeting watery graves!"

Sea Rescue Command asked him for his exact location and he provided it, saying his ship was in distress to the west of the Baltic Sea island of Bornholm.

The command unit assured him help was on the way and, not realizing that the capsizing freighter was likely to be next to a rubber ducky, dispatched two rescue ships to the area where the "captain" said he was stranded. They searched in earnest for one and a half hours.

Baffled over the absence of sinking ships in the area identified, the authorities decided to investigate further, putting a trace on the man's calls, which eventually led them to his home.

Presumably out of the bath by that point, he admitted to his hoax. Police fined him £900 for the expense they incurred over the false alarm.

Mothers (and Everyone Else) against Drunk Dialling

More and more people are getting gassed and picking up the phone in the wee small hours of the morning to, say, berate a boss, inform their ex-girlfriend/ex-boyfriend exactly what kind of greatness they are missing, or call an all-night radio talk show (this last is encouraged). Accordingly, Virgin Mobile in Australia now offers a service whereby users can block calls from people they think might drink and dial between 12 A.M. and 6 A.M. (Virgin.com.aus)

V

Acts of Passion and Other Poor Excuses

Booze is a great motivator. Indeed, it has had a hand in putting a good many of us here on this earth. What starts out as a drunken two-eyed wink, a strut across a sticky barroom floor and a call for "one more cocktail for the lady" does on occasion end up in a bouncing bundle of inconvenience (i.e., you).

Those who have childhood memories of their father looking to an empty bottle of Wild Turkey on a shelf, then to their mother who sleeps in a separate bedroom, then to his other six kids before finally holding his head in his hands and softly weeping will be familiar with the ability booze has to drive us to actions that we would not otherwise take and that we may, at some point, regret.

And this is certainly nothing new. For the ancient Romans (and their modern-day exemplars in all-inclusive resorts), wine served not as a sacrament, tonic and nourishment, but as something that gave people stuff to talk about pre-orgy at all those toga parties. When our forefathers realized that our foremothers became that much more appealing when one or both parties were under its spell, boozing and matters of the heart became inextricably linked.

By freeing people from their inhibitions, boozing also often loosens tongues—stay sober at a crowded bar on any Friday night, eavesdrop on those around you and you are sure to be introduced to a world full of lies. You may even tell a few fibs yourself, maybe about exactly how important you are at the firm where you dash around all day with a box of day-olds in one hand and your supervisor's Daytimer in the other. Or perhaps you recount experiences to friends that you might very well have had if you lived the kind of wild life that the people who write in to the sex-advice columns do.

Many such actions have been blamed squarely on the bottle, and while we certainly acknowledge that daiquiris taken before and steadily after the noon hour may not bring the best results by the time your name is called to deliver the keynote address at an early-evening Shriners convention, there seems to be something else at play with those featured in Acts of Passion and Other Poor Excuses. After all, is it strictly an alcohol-fuelled afternoon that inspires a man to settle a feud with a neighbour by stealing a prized teddy bear from her porch?

Whatever strange mental states are already an issue here, booze pushes people like the heroes of this section that one step further—convincing them to finally wreak vengeance on someone for whom they've long held a grudge, to pursue that forbidden romance (public displays of affection between man and inflatable doll are, as a rule, frowned upon) or to tell extravagant lies regarding one's own identity with the unblinking bluster that only strong drink can bring. And for that, we onlookers, unlike their victims, are grateful.

14
The Intoxicated Avengers

Where vice is, vengeance follows.

—SCOTTISH PROVERB

Hard-Headed Hard Hat

THE IRISH TIMES, NOVEMBER 1994

There's a lot more to being a bartender than the technical aspects of the job like knowing how much Bailey's to dump into a Cement Mixer (a jigger's worth will do you nicely thar, b'y) or whether Finlandia Vodka is actually required for a Crazy Finn (in a purist's eyes and possibly those of a Finn's: yes).

Bartending is a social job and requires some knowledge of human behaviour, particularly that of the loathsome variety. You have to be able to spot the telltale signs of intoxication, for example, and remember if you've actually poured that stinking guy in the trench coat 4 beers or 12.

And if unwittingly you've served someone to the point where they are violently drunk and proclaiming that they are ready to drop those closest to them like shit from the proverbial tall horse, then you need to know how to cool things down.

That said, no bartending guru *ever* could have predicted the reaction of a pub-goer when he was unceremoniously tossed from a Kilkenny pub. The building worker, angry at being booted out of the tavern, came back later that day very, very heavily armed. At the helm of a telescopic crane that he had procured from a neighbouring construction site, he told everyone who was listening, which at that point was absolutely everyone, that he would lower the boom on the pub if he was not given another drink.

Fortunately for the publican, the man did not go through with his threat. He later pleaded guilty to interfering with a mechanical vehicle and being drunk and disorderly.

In-Laws and Outlaws

Deutsche Presse-Agentur (Germany), August 2001;
PAP Polish News Agency, August 2001

Mothers-in-law have a place in most people's hearts somewhere between pit vipers and repo men. Marriages have been destroyed because women marry men who have been overexposed to maternal love and are forced to deal with their mothers' suffocating, psychotic machinations and frequent phone calls "just to make sure that hussy is taking good care of my Jimmy." Conversely, spouses who have no regard for their special someone's folks and want to excommunicate them like a drunk-on-power pope are no better.

Such relations can become tenser than a rope dangling a rock climber at fat camp; however, before either party considers retaliatory measures it is best to examine the legality of the planned course of action. A 52-year-old woman had reached the end of her tether as far as her mother-in-law was concerned and wanted to exact some revenge, but her plan landed her in the drunk-tank with charges pending.

The daughter-in-law was soused, bitter and looking to get even with her meddling mother-in-law. Taking a suitcase, she wrote the word BOMB on it in big letters and brought it to the old woman's nursing home. Approaching incredulous office staff, she handed off the suitcase, said there was a bomb inside and left instructions that it be hand-delivered to her mother-in-law's room.

Police were immediately summoned and, after they had a closer look, they found that the suitcase contained no explosives. But meanwhile the bomb scare had forced the evacuation of the home's 102 residents.

The hard-done-by daughter-in-law was picked up by authorities within a couple of hours of the incident, still drunk. They left her to cool her heels in the joint while they seriously considered bringing charges of terrorism against her.

A Saucy Fellow

DEUTSCHE PRESSE-AGENTUR (GERMANY), SEPTEMBER 2000

For habitual drinkers the phrase "don't let the door hit you on the ass on the way out" spoken by one's employer is not exactly alien to the ear. Compared with holding down a bar stool or palming a pint, staying gainfully employed is a far trickier sort of business.

Once they are given the gate, some might take the time to reflect on their lives and the sorry, unemployment-line direction being taken, or they might, like a certain pizza chef in Vienna, vent their frustrations in a grand, messy display of vengeance.

The 41-year-old pizza maker was shown the door by his employer for repeatedly boozing it up while on the job. The pizza chef proceeded to uncork a few bottles of wine and spend the day getting increasingly drunk and, with temperatures rising higher than those of a pizza oven, increasingly angry. By the evening, he had decided to pay an unwelcome after-hours visit to his former employer's restaurant.

Breaking in through a window, the drunken pie-maker went on a one-hour rampage in the restaurant, smashing 80 eggs against the walls and on the floor, throwing rice and vegetables all over the place, breaking every glass and plate he could get his hands on and smearing the tablecloths with overly generous servings of ketchup, thereby conferring some sense of the quality of the establishment. For his final hurrah he tried to set a pile of old newspapers and restaurant bills ablaze. Fortunately for the restaurant owner, they only smouldered and did not catch fire—protecting the crazed pizza maker from an arson rap.

His impromptu redecorating efforts resulted in US$4,500 worth of damages and earned him a six-month jail sentence. Still, he showed little remorse during the trial, telling the judge that the raid had left him exhausted and that afterwards he had enjoyed a restful night's sleep.

Teddy Bear Scare

DAILY TELEGRAPH (AUSTRALIA), DECEMBER 1999

"What are you in for?" must be the all-time cliché ice-breaker for those socially awkward moments when you're trying to suss out your new prison cellmate's criminal predilections. If you're the one asking the question, the terms *cannibal* or *sexual sadist* may race through your worried mind. If however you're the one answering the question, then it's in your best interest to try to garner grudging respect from your fellow Big House bunkees by giving a response like "hanging a corrupt warden." It could make your stay a little less unpleasant. On the other hand, less respect may be accorded to you for having defrauded the elderly in a boiler-room telemarketing scam.

One can only imagine the look on his fellow inmates' faces when, in response to "What are you in for?" a certain Australian replied, "Assault ... on a teddy bear."

Teddy bear assault is, to the best of our knowledge, not a chargeable offence anywhere in the world (we're waiting for a call back from Belgium to confirm this); the arrest of the man in question, we'll call him Mr. C, was due to a violation of a restraining order placed against him—during which he assaulted a stuffed animal.

Mr. C had feuded with his downstairs neighbour ever since she phoned police on him and his de facto (common-law) wife during a loud domestic argument. He soon began harassing the woman downstairs—crooning in her garden late at night, ringing her doorbell at all hours—and as a result she won a restraining order against him.

Then one day a drunken Mr. C caught sight of his neighbour's prized teddy bear, named Greg, which had been left on her veranda. The team colours of the St. George–Illawarra rugby team are red and white; however, Greg, unfortunately, was green and white, incensing Mr. C, a stalwart St. George–Illawarra supporter.

Mr. C grabbed Greg and began pounding him with a closed fist, literally punching his face in, and shouting: "It should be red and white!"

Thinking that Mr. C was going to send Greg to that great stuffed animal bin in the sky, his neighbour screamed for him to stop, the bear being a childhood keepsake given to her years ago by her now deceased father after a trying hospital stay.

Mr. C would hear nothing of her pleas for mercy on behalf of Greg and didn't stop until police showed up at the scene. Since he was already out on probation on other charges, Mr. C earned himself an additional five weeks in the slammer for violating his neighbour's restraining order with the teddy bear bashing.

Having a Ball

THE GUARDIAN (U.K.), JANUARY 2005

A lesser writer would say it was a "ballsy" move on her part, but given our predilection for aiming slightly higher than the belt, the case of the jilted woman who admitted to ripping off her ex-lover's testicle will be left in your capable hands.

The pair was at a party in Merseyside when the drunken woman, 24, told her ex, 37, that she wanted to discuss their relationship. During the course of the ensuing discussion, she offered him sex, and he refused.

When her advances were spurned, the jilted woman, in her best hell-hath-no-fury fashion, attacked her ex-boyfriend, grabbing his face and pulling him to the floor. Unfortunately for the poor fellow he was clad only in shorts, putting his family jewels in peril, prone to a slot-machine-lever-like downward tug.

His crazed former lover cleverly tried to hide the offending gonad by putting it in her mouth before dropping it. Another party-goer conscripted to make a most unorthodox delivery handed the maimed man the testicle, saying: "That's yours."

Indeed it was, though it never quite would be again. Doctors were unable to reattach it.

15
I Just Called to Say I've Been Drinking: Tales of Romance

Give me a woman who loves beer and I will conquer the world.

—KAISER WILHELM

Can I Buy You a Drink, Doll-Face?

COURIER-MAIL (AUSTRALIA), JANUARY 1985

An Australian man whose charms may not have been advanced enough to procure a date with any carbon-based life form claims to have no recollection of sneaking off to romance a less animated escort—an inflatable doll from a local sex shop.

The man (we'll call him Mr. B, not to prevent him from suffering any undue embarrassment but because of a brief chat with a lawyer) spent the day getting drunk at a hotel before he made his way into town to bust into the sex shop and abscond with the doll.

In sentencing Mr. B, the judge remarked on how improbable it was that he was able to drive in such a drunken condition from his hotel to the sex shop without being detected.

Since he had no previous criminal record, and possibly taking into account the public shaming that Mr. B received at the hands of the press, the judge did not record a conviction.

Mr. B said he was "shocked" by the incident and that he had no recollection of what happened. As a result he has since given up the ol' nectar, though his predilection for women who blow up instantly rather than after you marry them may be ongoing, as the inflatable doll was never recovered.

DISHONOURABLE MENTION
A Striptease, If You Please

In Estonia, a woman pulled over by the cops on suspicion of driving under the influence didn't get the reaction she'd hoped for when, in a move that was captured on police video (and no doubt replayed until the grainy VHS spool wore out), she performed a roadside striptease to get out of a ticket. It was a well-informed manoeuvre given that the fine in those parts is roughly equal to a month's pay.

This last-ditch effort was carried out, not surprisingly, after the motorist failed the Breathalyzer. The two cops who were treated to the show were offered a more private performance for afterward, but apparently refused. (Associated Press, October 2004; CBS News, October 2004; FOX News, October 2004)

The Hell with It All, Geritol Lovers

REUTERS, MARCH 2006

A classic poem on the effects of aging, often (we think falsely) attributed to Dr. Seuss, goes something like this: "The golden years are here at last / I cannot see, I cannot pee / I cannot chew, I cannot screw / The golden years are here at last / The golden years can kiss my ass!"

A couple of aging pensioners in Milan would have taken exception to the third line of that piece of verse, enjoying as they were the fruit of frolicking.

Police first took notice of a vehicle zigzagging along—nothing unusual about that, until, that is, they pulled the car over. The sight they were then to behold was one for which police academy training had not prepared them: almost 130 years of aged flesh in all its sagging, drooping glory.

The car's jerky movements had been caused by the woman, 70, trying to have sex with the naked driver, a man who was 11 years her junior.

The police undoubtedly averted their eyes while the couple dressed, then tested the driver's blood-alcohol level. They found that this aging Italian stallion, who still had some gas in his own tank, was quite gassed himself: on a Breathalyzer he blew over three times the legal limit.

The arresting officer blamed the drunken, amorous joyride on several drinks consumed at lunchtime, one thing leading to another. Asked if the couple were married, he said he wasn't sure, though he clearly doubted the possibility, telling Reuters news agency, "Married people would never do something like this."

Marquis de Sod

HERALD SUN (AUSTRALIA), JANUARY 1992

In British peerage a marquis ranks below a duke and above an earl—esoteric, seldom-heard terms in these parts with the exception of the doo-wop hit "Duke of Earl," apparently about an unrelenting sovereign prince. While none of these terms can match the mellifluous Grand Poobah or the weighty designation Head Honcho, they nonetheless confer a certain eminence. But before you scour your family tree looking to find blood bluer than a Heimlich recipient's face, consider for a moment the following.

In a wasted attempt to find his girlfriend, one such aristocrat was arrested by police early in the morning buzzing intercoms and banging on random doors in a block of flats. The liquored-up lord was completely unaware that the woman had since moved.

According to a local resident, who had been roused from her dream state by the royal kafuffle at 5 A.M., "There was no way anyone was going to let him in at that hour. He was obviously very intoxicated."

The marquis, despite being heir to a $250-million fortune, was familiar with jurisprudence, having done a stint in the coop for drug offences in the 1980s. During his most recent stretch he had attempted to rekindle romance with prison-penned jottings smuggled to his paramour.

These *belles lettres,* however, did not sit too kindly with his wife, who likely regrets standing by him while he did his time.

Manchester United

OTTAWA CITIZEN, OCTOBER 1999

Not to burst their tech bubbles, but being involved in optical network management, multi-protocol routers and ethernet switches can't vie with white-water rafting instructor, private investigator, topless gentlemen's club bouncer and helicopter pilot for the "most exciting job on the planet."

If the intrigue brought to the accounting profession from the scandals at Enron et al. affected them as well, high-tech workers wouldn't have to make up their own fun to convince people that sitting all day in a cubicle with a slide rule, or whatever it is they do, is the zenith of exhilaration.

A married female sales director, perhaps doing whatever it takes for that set of steak knives and a fat year-end bonus, was arrested in Manchester after getting bladdered and canoodling with another married passenger on a jet. Unfortunately, the two were not married to each other. According to reports, the woman, hopefully after requesting extra blankets from airline staff, was caught in a position of genuflection that made Monica Lewinsky a household name and a punch line.

Cabin crew asked the woman, a sales director from Maidenhead, and too old, by implication, for the authors to make the obvious crack here, and her new-found gentleman caller to stop, and they did not.

The pair was released on bail and scheduled to appear in court to face charges of public lewdness and more.

DISHONOURABLE MENTION
You've Got Male—More Suburban Shenanigans

There are two basic rules for sending things through the mail: a) Do not send anything that is alive, and, on a related note, b) Do not send anything that is dead. There are countless cases in which someone lands "the big one," wraps it up and by the time it's opened, the poor trout is putrid and beginning to smell.

Here's a fishy package of another sort. A Renfrewshire man, in the midst of what his lawyer dubbed a "drunken escapade," thrust his erect penis through a woman's letterbox. The man, who was arrested and admitted to public indecency with Freudian overtones, was also said to have uttered an obscene remark, presumably in case the woman was blind and missed the full weight of the gesture. (*The Sun,* U.K., February 2004)

16

I'm Not Really a Drunk, I Just Play One on TV: Alibis and Alter Egos

I envy people who drink—at least they know who to blame everything on.

—OSCAR LEVANT

Catch Me 'Cause I'm Crocked

MIAMI HERALD, SEPTEMBER 1997

Having a recognizable name or holding a position of power has certain perks. You get freebie meals from restaurateurs who hope you'll one day turn a blind eye to their flagrant health-code violations and, best of all, you get access to places that work hard to shut out your average slob. Who among us wouldn't gladly give up our table in a crowded restaurant and finish our meal on a cold wintry sidewalk so that a visiting luminary who just stumbled in with no reservations could have a seat? It is a sign of respect for success in our society.

When doling out these favours though, it is important to make certain that the VIP in question is, in fact, *very important*. Theatre managers in Laguna Beach, California, learned this the hard way when a man claiming to be the mayor of Fort Lauderdale, Florida, approached them for tickets to a performance of the Pageant of the Masters exhibition.

The performance was sold out; however, the manager of the theatre told the *Miami Herald* that "if the Queen of England were to come to the window, we would have a ticket," and presumably meant this to apply to the far less noteworthy mayor of Fort Lauderdale.

Theatre staff thought something was amiss when the supposed mayor showed them his driver's licence—which gave his address as Plantation, Florida, rather than Fort Lauderdale. Satisfied with his response that Plantation was a suburb of Fort Lauderdale, staff gave him excellent seats for the performance.

The fraudulent mayor proceeded to get "exceedingly drunk" during the performance, and after the final curtain, nearly caused an accident by speeding out of the parking lot.

The next morning the theatre manager looked into the matter and eventually tracked down the office of the actual mayor. He discovered that although the mayor had been at a pub opening that night, he had not left the state of Florida and, to the credit of his constituents, was not responsible for putting on a drunken display at a theatre in California.

DISHONOURABLE MENTION
He'sh an Imposhtor, Mish Moneypenny

When giving out fictitious names to authorities it is best to stick with ones that could conceivably be true, or at the very least, that of your worst enemy who had it coming to him anyway. A teen from rural Ireland was arrested for causing a ruckus outside of an area nightclub, swearing at the arresting officers, and when asked to provide his name, telling them he was James Bond.

A judge later asked him if he knew who had created the character of James Bond. When the teen answered that he had no idea who wrote the original Bond books (or presumably that such books existed), the judge replied: "Exactly, any half intelligent person would be able to answer that, but you cannot." He fined the youth and banned this 000 from attending his favourite dance spot for a year.

Oh, and after consulting with a confused but helpful telephone operator just now, we are reasonably sure it was Ian Fleming who penned those books. (*The Corkman,* U.K., March 2006)

Badge of Dishonour

KCAL TV (U.S.), MARCH 2006; CBS2.COM, MARCH 2006

The City of Angels, so called because in many of its more ramshackle neighbourhoods you may feel compelled to utter a silent appeal to your guardian one, is not exactly known for its cheery, walkable streets.

While you're unlikely to find any common ground with your Blood or Cripp antagonist (save perhaps for an enthusiasm for puffy jackets), you might helpfully suggest "Don't forget my PIN there, friend" in the hope of avoiding the kind of beating for which the city has become so famous.

With the reputation of even the city's police force not being (how can we put this delicately and avoid making more enemies than we already have) as sparkling as it could be, a suspected drunk driver's claim that he was a detective on the force might not immediately have aroused any suspicion. What may have tipped off the cops who pulled him over was that the purported detective was rolling around in a Porsche—a vehicle whose costly high-tech German engineering is out of the range of all but the most cleverly corrupt gumshoes.

The would-be cop flashed his badge and had the presence of mind to mention that he worked at the Downey division office, which actually exists. Before anyone could utter "His story checks out, boss," the driver's story began to unravel like the lining of a cheap suit. The man admitted that he had purchased the badge on the Internet so that he could "impress women." He did not elaborate as to exactly what kind of woman would be wooed by police credentials, bogus or otherwise.

DISHONOURABLE MENTION
The Secret Policeman's Other Ball

Impersonating a police officer is a chargeable offence, which is why most officers are told to hang on to their official gear and never lend it out.

An officer working with an Australian police force made such a mistake by lending out one of his old uniforms to a buddy who needed a convincing getup for a Halloween party. In a situation that seemed to have been run by the sitcom logic of "anything that can go wrong definitely will," his friend left the party blasted and hailed a cab on the street. No cab came, and with the effects of the drink taking their toll, the knock-off cop passed out in the gutter.

Passersby saw the man and were alarmed, thinking that it was an officer in distress and quite possibly dead in the street. But they quickly discovered the man's true identity, and later he was charged an A$300 fine for impersonating an officer. (*Herald Sun,* Australia, June 2003)

Here's Mud in Your (Glass) Eye!

REUTERS, JANUARY 2006

When impersonating someone, mastering the subtleties is important, but mastering the grossly obvious is crucial. As anyone who has ever tried to sneak into a bar with a fake ID will tell you, it's vital that in your new identity as "Larry Tillman" you are within six inches of his height, within five years either way of his age, and at least relatively close on the skin-colour continuum.

A German man who was pulled over by police for driving drunk in the western city of Bochum attempted to avoid having any charges added to his record by giving police the name of a close acquaintance of his, along with all pertinent details.

Police ran a check on the information the man provided and all appeared to be in order—until one of the officers noticed a unique point on the record of the man on file: he was registered as having a glass eye.

Growing suspicious and wanting to test out the veracity of the man's claim, the officers shone a flashlight in his eye, which immediately responded to the stimulus, thus revealing the man's lie.

In response to being found out, the drunk offered an excuse that would have brought a tear to his good friend's glass eye, saying that in what would have been a spectacular breakthrough in medical science, he had once had a glass eye but was back to the genuine article again.

After police established the identity of the man, who it could be said had an eye for trouble, they also found that he had been driving without a licence because of a previous offence.

Steel-Wheels Tour

THE ADVERTISER (AUSTRALIA), APRIL 1997

Drunk driving laws do not as a rule apply to the operation of motorized wheelchairs or scooters, but perhaps they should. You might agree if you've ever been at the local mall and been forced to leap out of the way of one, piloted by some guy with a fur cap and the national flag flapping in the breeze who's bearing down on you with *Days of Thunder*–like speed to beat you to a Boxing Day sale.

An Australian man showed just how out-of-control matters can get when the steel-wheels set get into the tipple. The motorized-wheelchair-bound man had just returned from his local pub after sinking, as he told *The Advertiser* newspaper, "the usual eight or nine beers" when he decided to take his chair out for a ride on city streets.

By the time police arrived on the scene, this easy rider was barrelling down the road against oncoming traffic, drinking a can of beer—with his negligee-clad wife at the controls in his lap. When police approached him and tried to get the man to pull over, the drunken ironsides cursed at them and tried to run down the officers. By the time police did manage to corral the man and bring him in to face charges of disorderly behaviour and resisting arrest, he refused to answer any questions and told them his name was Donald Duck.

Once matters had settled, "Donald Duck" broke his silence and spoke with a local newspaper, defending his actions that night by saying that he was "just teaching the missus to drive." She needed to learn how to operate the chair, he said, because he was a man who enjoyed his booze often to the point that he was incapable of operating the chair himself, and he didn't always have the cash to fork out for taxi fare.

Let Me Give You a Ride Home

Sixty-one percent of adults in the United States (122 million people) have served designated driver duty at one time or another or have been driven home by a designated driver. (Data Development Corporation, 2004)

Belligerent Drunk Man's Not-So-Super Powers

GAINESVILLE SUN, NOVEMBER 2005; COURTTV.COM, NOVEMBER 2005

Superman was never much of a beer drinker or a frequenter of bars and that, presumably, is because of his otherworldly metabolic rate. To get Superman drunk, it would probably take enough alcohol to fill one of the smaller Great Lakes—or at the very least more than your average Metropolis barkeep would have in his stockroom. Batman, cursed with the limitations of a human, also rarely drinks, causing many a liquid courage–filled barfly to venture that, if it came to it, "I could take Batman."

A partier attending a Halloween bash dressed himself as a super-hero of sorts, "Belligerent Drunk Man," and while BDM has never graced the pages of DC Comics, his exploits on this day did make newspaper headlines. To complete his superhero getup, the man wore a sweatsuit, a belt made out of the tops of beer cans and, the topper, a large Superman-like "BDM" emblazoned across his chest.

Fellow party-goers were enjoying BDM's clever costume and self-effacing style, until he underwent a superhero-like transformation—not unlike that which turned paltry Bill Bixby into hulking Lou Ferrigno (or Eric Bana into an unconvincing computer-generated mess)—brought on, as his name suggests, by lots of booze.

A tussle broke out at this point between BDM and another party-goer outfitted as the Green Lantern. Now, as comic book aficionados know, the Green Lantern, a staple of DC Comics since the 1950s, is a character with incredible power bestowed by the sacred Green Lantern ring. However, in order to harness this power one must have perfect control over one's mind, something that late into the night at a drinking party, you are unlikely to have.

When police arrived to break up the battle he was having with BDM, the Green Lantern went on to attack the officers. His status in the Justice League fell into doubt when his legendary powers were not enough to overcome a pepper spraying at the hands of police.

VI

You Animal!

Studies have shown that given a choice, and in no less natural a setting than a research lab, animals will quite readily consume alcohol at a rate that would put the teetering guy at the end of the bar to shame.

These tests, which involve rats depressing a lever in a cage to allow the steady flow of alcohol in a kind of rodent "happy hour," reveal that our mammalian cousins have little trouble engaging in the type of behaviour that in humans usually culminates in episodes such as those chronicled in this book. Moreover, rats, like the great rock stars of the early 1970s, will self-administer both cocaine and booze until death, pressing the lever more frantically than a pensioner at a slot machine if they are left socially isolated.

Skeptics point out, however, that with these sorry beasts being confronted by the discomfort of isolation in an "Ivy League pet store," prodded with various needles and intermittently fed to snakes, it is hardly a surprise that they would turn to stimulus boosts. Regardless, the reward for dulling oneself with drink and drugs is dopamine, which surges through both our brains and those of our animal friends. In Crapulent Critters we found that man and beast have more in common than perhaps even Darwin could have imagined when he went poking around in the Galapagos Islands. Like the alcoholic dog living with those college frat guys, these beasts have a strong propensity for the drink.

Man Bites Dog and Dog Bites Back features the age-old battle between man and beast and shows how the latter has a much better chance of victory if the former is off his trosh during the contest. Here we see animals getting one over on people when they attempt to do things as foolish as, say, climbing into a bear cage at the zoo, and learn what can happen when you keep a chimpanzee as a personal pet and forget to lock the liquor cabinet.

17
Crapulent Critters: Beastly Behaviour

No animal ever invented anything as bad as drunkenness—or so good as drink.

—G.K. Chesterton

Draft Horses

Press Association (U.K.), July 1992

Venerated in mall concourses everywhere, lovingly rendered in black velvet or adorning giant beach towels, the noble horse is part of our common mythology.

From Silver, the Lone Ranger's ride, to "White Feller," the moniker of choice for Tonto's steed in those simpler, less ironic times, to the crazy hijinks of talking horse Mr. Ed, who would comically swipe apples from the neighbour's yard week after insufferable week, they have also been among man's very best buddies.

Unfortunately, some horse owners take this buddy relationship too far, and such was the case when two horse owners brought their steed for a pint at a pub in Hampton West, London.

Patrons and staff were treated to a barnyard stench, and likely thinking that the toilet had backed up for the umpteenth time, took no notice.

It wasn't until Dolly the horse buckled the pub's door frames and sent reinforced glass door panels flying that the surprised and then increasingly agitated drinkers desperately shoved her out—only to have the thirsty mare return again 15 minutes later for another round.

A labourer and a retired horse trainer appeared in court to defend their actions. The horse trainer said that he had been drunk at the time of the incident and that people there had fed the horse with chips and given her a pint. He said that if a bloke had had too much to drink, Dolly would take him home. "She's a good old horse you can trust," he said.

This statement, which likely had magistrates questioning the man's sobriety during the court proceedings, was backed up by that of his lawyer, a legal lion who pointed out that the horse had "no criminal culpability."

Riding on a Horse with No Blame

On February 1, 2006, lawmakers in South Dakota passed a bill that would exempt horses and bikes from drunk driving laws. Thus, in that state, using them to get home after a night on the town is perfectly legal. (AP, February 2006)

Drunk Dogs and Englishmen

QUEENSLAND NEWS PRESS (AUSTRALIA), JULY 1999; AGENCE FRANCE-PRESSE
(FRANCE), JULY 1999; DEUTSCHE PRESS-AGENTUR (GERMANY), JULY 1999

Since the age of 18, the Queen has kept four Pembroke corgis with
her at all times and is said to dote on them: they are even given little
rubber boots to protect their paws from the gravel at Buckingham
Palace. Despite this loving attention and the fact that these dogs
have their own quarters within palace walls, they are notoriously
ill-tempered.

The Queen once brought in a "dog psychiatrist" to try to cure
the corgis of their tendency to clamp their jaws down on the ankles
of strangers as well as to fight with one another. Primal scream
therapy or whatever the dog psychiatrist tried did not cure the
dogs of their nasty dispositions and he left palace officials with an
eardrum-bursting rape-whistle to blow whenever the dogs started
to fight.

Not surprisingly the dogs are regarded as a nuisance by some
royal household staff. Perhaps this was what prompted a staffer, 28,
then in his third year as one of the Queen's two personal 24-hour
on-call footmen, to make these majestic mutts the subject of a bit
of frivolity.

It was his "duty" as footman to feed the corgis on a daily basis in
accordance with a vet-vetted diet. Reports say that at some point
while carrying out this charge, the footman decided to start pouring
gin and whisky into the dogs' water bowls and food.

As we all know, seeing drunk dogs—particularly ones with low
centres of gravity on short little legs—is funny indeed.

The Queen, however, was horrified, and most definitely not amused when she found out the reason why her dogs wanted to join her for bedtime toddies. She stripped the footman of his lofty rank and cut his pay.

Sadly, one of the corgis, Pharos, went on to meet a grisly death at the paws of Princess Anne's bull terrier. The other three dogs, Kelpe, Swift and Emma, have by all accounts dried out completely.

Polly Want a Pint?

Courier-Mail (Australia), July 1985; *Daily Mirror* (U.K.), July 1985

A parrot walks into a bar and asks the barman: "Do you have any bread?"

The barman replies: "No, this is a pub. We sell beer."

The parrot then asks: "Do you have any bread?"

To which the barman again replies, "No."

The parrot then says, yet again (testing the patience of listeners, indicated by the pained expression on their faces as they realize the payoff won't be nearly worth the time it takes to get through this): "Do you have any bread?"

The barman says: "Listen, if you ask me one more time if I've got any bread I'll nail your f—ing beak to the bar, okay?"

The parrot looks shocked and asks: "Do you have any nails?"

The barman, throwing that cloth that barmen and barwomen are always bandying about, shouts, *"No!"*

To which the parrot responds: "Well then, do you have any bread?"

You'd think the mere existence of such awful jokes would have resulted in the banning of a parrot from a pub in Somerset, England.

It was Fred the polluted parrot's own unruly behaviour, however, that resulted in his being banned from the bar where he had been the acting mascot. The bird, which the *Daily Mirror* took the trouble of pointing out was "of the feathered variety," decided to switch allegiances between beer and hard liquor, and as has been the case with many of his flightless fellow drinkers, the move had a distinct effect on his disposition.

After switching to rum and cola, he began sipping customers' drinks, and if anybody was unwise enough to give him any lip about it, the winged wastrel would peck them for their troubles. When the bar closed for the night, a drunken Fred would cavort around sending bottles crashing to the ground and setting off the burglar alarm.

His landlord, having already tolerated more from Fred than he likely would have from customers who paid for their drinks and did not shit on the bar, was ultimately forced to ban him.

Teaching a Small Dog New Tricks

NBC5.COM, MARCH 2006; WMAQ TV CHICAGO, MARCH 2006

It used to be that a dog was a boy's best friend—back when Timmy was getting dropped into wells and his only hope for escape was not the backward people that ran his town, but his faithful dog Lassie. Those days are long gone and now dogs have become the best friend, or at least the most favoured accoutrement, of women with too much disposable income on their hands who stuff some pitiable pooch into a handbag that matches their shoes.

Chihuahuas in particular, having weathered the Taco Bell era, are now selected for this dubious distinction. They are bred to be about 6 to 9 inches tall and roughly 4 pounds, the perfect size for would-be Paris Hiltons (and unhappily they do exist) to schlep around.

Dogs this size face risks, however, especially if their owners are not in tiptop physical condition and suddenly roll over on the sofa, or if the dog is exposed to an angry raccoon or a bigger dog such as, well, any other dog out there.

A woman with a fondness for keeping one of these ankle-nippers with her was brought up on drunk driving, animal cruelty and child endangerment charges after she showed up at her son's elementary school in Illinois completely wasted, with her trusted little tail-wagger at her side, equally wasted.

The woman said that a seizure her dog was having (presumably due to the low-alcohol tolerance of such a tiny animal) caused her to lose control and drive her vehicle up onto the sidewalk in front of the school.

The dog spent the night at an emergency veterinary clinic undergoing detox while the woman pleaded her case to the police.

DISHONOURABLE MENTION
The Buck Stops Here

The elk is a peaceful animal, but will rise in defence of its own in the face of a threat. Such a threat took the form of a bunch of retirees in Sweden.

Cops were called to their retirement home, not to break up a booze-fuelled canasta punch-up, but to deal with erratically behaving elk, dear me. At first the fuzz managed to drive away the beasts, a mother and her calf, who were completely bluttered on fermented apples (presumably ones that had been left outside), but then the raging fauna turned on their human masters and cops were forced to call for backup—a hunter with a dog.

"It's better to get rid of the apples from the home," noted the police commissioner, in a case of hindsight being a 20-gauge shotgun. (*The Local,* Sweden, November 2005; UPI, November 2005)

Who's Afraid of the Big Bad Wolf? Everyone

THE TELEGRAPH (U.K.), DECEMBER 2004; *EDINBURGH NEWS,* DECEMBER 2004

We are all accustomed to nasty neighbours—you know, the ones upstairs who trudge around in work boots in the wee hours of the morning, cough up lung matter like a coal miner with hay fever, or vacuum their venetian blinds as you slowly sip your morning coffee, plugs in ears, perusing the funny pages.

A drunken yob and budding lycanthrope earned the distinction of being the only human included in this chapter by "screaming and wailing like a werewolf" at the top of his lungs. A full moon was not the impetus for this carrying on; rather, it was inspired by his having watched the horror flick *An American Werewolf in London* over and over again.

The man, a 28-year-old Scottish villager, a good decade older than the age at which you'd expect someone to suspend their disbelief in ancient German folklore, was found guilty of breaching an anti-social behaviour order after making the lives of his neighbours miserable. He'd urinate out the window of his first-floor flat and moan all through the night, intermittently banging on glass and playing ear-splitting tunes. The man was also found leaping from a ladder onto his couch and doing a bizarre dance with his Christmas tree.

Eventually, amid neighbours' complaints of "werewolf noises," he was hauled into court for his actions.

A police constable noted that his behaviour "all came from drink," and expressed relief that this "Wolfman Jack-ass" would spend the Christmas holidays behind bars.

Medium Rare Birds

REUTERS, FEBRUARY 1995; ITAR-TASS NEWS AGENCY (RUSSIA), FEBRUARY 1995

In Victorian days, zoos were places for exotic animals to be caged, gawked at and poked with sharp sticks by inquisitive kids, people needing to prove to themselves and the animals who rules the world. Apart from private joints run by eccentric millionaires who pride themselves on having their own dancing gibbon, most public zoos around the world are improving their reputations by focusing on ecological preservation and acting as a tool to educate the public about the wonders of the wild kingdom. Still, the safety and preservation of the animals within individual zoos depend on the professionalism of their keepers.

Workers at a Siberian zoo had just received their wages, and in typical payday fashion they made a liquor run. Unfortunately, they then did their best to drink up a fair portion of their wages as soon as the hooch was in hand—while still on duty at the zoo.

As they were celebrating, a fire had broken out in the nearby city of Prem and was, unbeknownst to the celebrating zoo workers, coming their way. Flames eventually reached a rare bird shelter and swept through it, flambéing hundreds of birds, including rare breeds of swans, guinea fowl and peacocks. The inferno continued to rage until guests at a neighbouring hotel phoned the fire brigade.

By the time firefighters arrived to extinguish the flames, they found the zookeepers drunk and staggering around the grounds, still completely oblivious to the feathered roast that was taking place on their watch.

18
Man Bites Dog and Dog Bites Back

Have an objective to give your bender a theme. For instance, stalking and killing a wild pig with a bowie knife.

—Hunter S. Thompson

Bear-ly Legal

Ananova.com (U.K.), July 2005

The struggle of man versus beast is an age-old one—Theseus and the Minotaur, Ahab and the great white whale, Papa Hemingway and anything whatsoever on land or in water—and to this tradition we can now add the tale of a drunken punter from Ukraine.

The 22-year-old was drinking at a bar when he began boasting to friends about his superhuman strength, saying that he possessed so much power that no mere mortal could test him, and that he would seek out suitable competition at the local zoo.

A while later, the trip to the zoo having apparently done nothing to sober the young champ up, he hand-picked what seemed to him at the time to be an opponent of equal measure: an 8-foot-tall, nearly 600-pound grizzly bear.

Seeing the beast in repose (and being crazy drunk) likely gave the man a false sense of self-confidence for the upcoming tussle and he climbed over the railing and jumped into the bear cage. Throwing down the gauntlet in this show-stopping bear-versus-man tilt, the man began beating the grizzly's hind legs.

Though nonplussed for the first few minutes, the grizzly soon realized the effrontery of what was taking place and proceeded to maul the young upstart within a standing eight-count of his life.

The bear's other cage-mates tried to join in the fracas before zookeepers intervened, saving the man from a mauling that, as anyone who has seen a dancing bear jamboree will agree, might have been considered entirely justified.

Feed You Later, Alligator

MOSNEWS.COM (RUSSIA), MARCH 2006

Heavily armed researchers, in an experiment that is about as likely to be replicated as one in which a drunk takes a leak on an electric fence, noted that the force exerted by an alligator's bite is nearly 3,000 pounds. This is roughly equivalent to one being stuck under a modest-sized pickup, with nary a circus strongman in sight.

A Russian company's mascot, a living and breathing reptilian force of nature rather than the cuddly one that adorns preppy garments on the links, was being treated to a drunken holiday meal when it snapped—literally.

The company's director, buoyed by boozy inspiration at a nationalistic holiday party, wanted to, in his words, "feed his handsome."

The gator, "Musya," who's lived in the company's Moscow head office for years (though unlikely drumming up much extra business by his presence), is typically fed through a special door to his cage. But with the liquor flowing freer than the Volga, the ripped executive ignored such safety precautions and recklessly flung open the main door to the bellicose beast's pen to offer him a sausage.

Musya, striking a blow for the proletariat everywhere, lunged forward, passed on the sausage that was offered to him and instead clamped down on the man's hand.

Luckily for the tanked executive, he managed to wriggle free from his "handsome's" grip, miraculously requiring only a trip to the hospital for tetanus shots.

Nearly Sunk Monk

QUEENSLAND NEWS PRESS, JANUARY 1985

Saint Francis of Assisi, perhaps wine-drunk from primordial plonk that predated Chianti, once told his companions, "Wait for me while I go preach to my sisters the birds," before striking out into the forest presumably to do just that.

According to legend, the saint also made peace with a vicious wolf in the city of Gubbio for whom the townspeople were an *il secondo* (main course) whenever they ventured into the mountains. "Brother wolf, I would like to make peace between you and the people," he uttered—though we're sure sounding more mellifluent in Italian—as the beast lay peacefully at his feet. The wolf was then brought into town and a deal struck between it and the townspeople, who promised to feed it regularly in exchange for the wolf's ceasing to devour any of them.

Years later, a brother at the San Romedio Monastery, established in honour of the saint, found himself stuck in a cage with an old bear named Charley, the monastery's mascot and one of dozens that have lived peaceably among the monks for centuries. Charley on this particular day was irritable, the result of having not slept well the night before. The unknowing brother started to clean out Charley's cage as he did every morning, and suddenly the bear readied itself to attack. At this point, the brother was, for all intents and purposes, "Friar Fucked."

As the panicked brother lay curled up on the floor, ready to meet his maker from this Ursa Major, another monk, channelling the spirit of Assisi, lobbed a bottle of monastery-made grappa into the cage.

Charley scarfed down the potent grape-based spirit and within minutes passed out.

"Thanks be to God that Charley liked grappa and drank the lot," noted the grateful monk. "It was not exactly the Holy Spirit, but the Lord works his wonders in many strange ways."

DISHONOURABLE MENTION
An Elephant Never Forgets

Most people are familiar with the idiom "the elephant in the room," referring to a problem that people simply choose to ignore despite its staring them right in the face. And it would seem that some elephants prefer to be ignored. Try as you might, it is impossible to pay no heed whatsoever to the "elephant in the room stomping some poor galoot to death."

According to a coroner's report in Australia, a comprehensive cautionary tale of the perils of running away to join the circus, an "act of intoxicated bravado" resulted in a 51-year-old horse groom buying a pine condo. Witnesses say the guy approached and touched Abu the elephant, and the pestered pachyderm pummelled him to the ground with his trunk. The beast then genuflected, crushing the horse handler like a peppercorn. (Australian Associated Press, November 1987)

Baked with Snake

DAILY TELEGRAPH (AUSTRALIA), MAY 2001

Gone are the days when on any major urban street corner you could find a man pumping out a tuneless cacophony of noise on his hurdy-gurdy street organ while a dandily attired monkey danced alongside him and collected spare change from passersby. Groups looking out for signs of animal cruelty have pretty much put an end to street performances using animals and have even given circus workers second thoughts about trying to squeeze Dumbo the elephant into a pair of size 36 pumps. In some places, however, sidewalk entertainers continue to employ animals in their acts—at their peril, as this story illustrates.

It was about 2:30 in the morning in Sydney when a snake "charmer" put on a display that did little to add credence to the title of his profession. Drunk and feeling nasty, the handler used his python to harass passersby—though not venomous, the carpet python is still a large and imposing-looking snake, not the kind of thing you want to come eye to eye with. The handler also began to bash his 4-foot-long python against a wall, which led to police being called to investigate allegations of both animal cruelty and harassment of onlookers.

When authorities arrived, they found the snake wrapped loosely around the handler's shoulders and—revenge time—the beast attempting to squeeze the bejesus out of him. The snake, which in the wild uses its tremendous strength to crush its prey, was presumably giving the man a quick lesson in the negative ramifications of cruelty to animals. Police and a large crowd watched agape as the man turned red and passed out. Police were eventually able to pry the snake off the neck of its drunken handler. When the man came to, presumably the worse for wear as a result of the oxygen recently denied his brain, he said he thought he was in Brisbane. The handler wasn't charged over the incident, but the snake, probably much to its relief, was given to wildlife authorities.

DISHONOURABLE MENTION
Snake Bite—Not the Cocktail

There are 36 possible ways to roll a pair of six-sided dice—for those of you headed to the casino after putting down this book. Rolling two ones, or "snake eyes," will guarantee your seat being vacated at the craps table and send you back to the bar to refill your drink and sob on a cocktail waitress's shoulder.

Understandably, "snake eyes" has come to signify bad luck, but not usually in such a literal sense as in the case of a 39-year-old Idaho man.

He and a group of similarly intellectually stunted compadres were taunting a pet rattlesnake in the back of the man's pickup, and trying to get the serpent drunk on beer.

The kibosh was put on their plans when the aggrieved snake bit the man, sending him to the hospital. A neuro-toxic rattlesnake bite is typically fatal if left untreated. The man remained in hospital overnight for observation.

His unsympathetic wife noted: "Sometimes I think he's 13." (Associated Press, July 1980)

This Chimp Ain't No Wimp

ASSOCIATED PRESS, AUGUST 1984; *NEW YORK TIMES,* AUGUST 1984

According to *Our Inner Ape,* by primatologist Frans de Waal, chimps are a lot less vegetarian than your average hippie would like to believe: they consume 35 different species of vertebrates, including monkeys and, if given the chance, the odd human baby. Yes, chimps are tough SOBs, possessing arm strength five times greater than that of even your most psychotic, 'roid-addled pro wrestler. And since they use their feet as arms, they have twice as many usable limbs with which to thrash you.

Given the potential devastation they are capable of unleashing, when making your exotic pet purchase it is advisable to leave the chimpanzee with the creepy person selling him and opt for something less dangerous—like a Russian bush pig or a few dozen rabid ferrets.

A family in Queens, New York, a place where behaviour is bad enough without throwing a raging anthropoid into the mix, learned just how unsuitable a chimp is as a domesticated pet.

The chimp in question, whose name, "Bongo," we will use without fear of legal repercussion, was left alone for the day and apparently not in a cage or locked in the former bedroom of a child now at university. Left to his own devices, Bongo began snooping around the family's domicile and eventually happened upon the liquor cabinet.

Bongo then displayed a level of evolution typically associated with your average 16-year-old humanoid when he pulled out a bottle of vodka, downed it, and washed that down with two bottles of beer.

Unfortunately, Bongo did not hold his liquor well, nor was he a nice drunk. Crashing through his owner's window, he ran out into the street and went, well, ape-shit, busting windows in the neighbourhood and biting a neighbour on the toe for good measure. Bongo was able to evade police for half an hour, until his owner got back and managed to convince him to return home—not to the jungle, mind you, but to his Queens apartment.

DISHONOURABLE MENTION
More Monkey Business

If a group of murderous monkeys were ever to attack, it'd be handy to have a young Chuck Heston at your side uttering that famous line of his that we would reproduce here were it not for copyright issues. Sadly, Heston was nowhere to be found when a group of marauding monkeys descended on a small village in the coastal Indian state of Orissa on the Bay of Bengal, guzzling pots of pana, a fermented alcohol- and marijuana-laced offering to the Hindu gods. Residents had prepared it for a religious festival that in no uncertain terms did not involve monkeys.

The pissed-up primates set upon the villagers, who drove them away with sticks and other makeshift weapons. In accordance with rules of engagement determining battles between simians and humans, monkeys that passed out from the potent concoction were returned to the forest unharmed. (Ananova.com; *Times of India,* April 2005)

VII

Celebrate Good Times: Getting Together and Falling Apart

At the birth of a child, many dads make a run to the liquor store, purchase a bottle of wine, promise themselves they're going to keep it as a way of commemorating the special day and end up polishing it off before the mewling babe has had his or her first bowel movement.

Each successive rite of passage in a person's life is likely to be tied to the heavy consumption of booze: from one's high-school prom when parents are wont to turn a blind eye to the cleaning bill sent to them by the tuxedo rental company, to the shotgun wedding that is the result of one too many vodka lemonades. Indeed, after we go to tap that great corn-whisky still in the sky, we can rest assured that people will continue to raise toasts to our name and mention the salvageable bits of our anecdotal legacy over drinks (until we are utterly forgotten, of course).

Celebrate Good Times focuses on the role that alcohol plays in life's special moments—and it is hardly a walk-on role for those chronicled here. This section contains stories of weddings that degenerate into drunken madness, which, given the popularity of the open bar, is to be expected. But then there are the fights at funerals and a riot involving men dressed as Santa Claus, as well as numerous other celebrations that turn from festive to ugly in a hurry once attendees are into their cups.

We're sure that those included in this section, particularly those in the chapter To Have and to Hold Up who are trying their best to keep their tales of infamy from the second wife or husband, would rather that the public's memory of their actions was as sketchy as their own. However, their tales, stories of people at different stages in their lives—about to get married, partying, dead—have been brought together as a testament on how to live and mark the great occasions, if not admirably, at least with some panache.

19
To Have and to Hold Up: Tying the Knot and Tying One On

Marriage is like putting your hand into a bag of snakes in the hope of pulling out an eel.

—LEONARDO DA VINCI

Getting Your Wedding Bells Rung

FOX NEWS, SEPTEMBER 2005; *NEW YORK DAILY NEWS,* SEPTEMBER 2005; *JOURNAL NEWS* (U.S.), SEPTEMBER 2005

Not since Marlon Brando showed his bare arse to 100 extras during the filming of the famous wedding scene in *The Godfather* has such an attack been launched on the sacred ceremony of marriage. A pier-six brawl at a big Italian-American wedding landed the groom and some of his wedding party in the honeymoon suite at the city jail, where the only wedding-night action might have involved the unsolicited advances of a drunk-tank bunkmate.

What would end up a donnybrook started off as a simple case of mistaken identity. Attendees at another wedding party underway at the same New York hotel mistook the brother of the groom for a photographer who had left them in the lurch. Rather than denying this easily refutable claim, the brother dispensed with formalities and punched his accuser in the head. One hundred people took up his cause, adding their own grappa-fuelled fists to the fracas.

By the time cops arrived on the scene, the fight had even spilled into an elevator.

A police spokesman called the incident "pure bedlam" and, displaying an adamantine-like grip on the obvious, added that he believed it may have been fuelled by alcohol.

The children's playground rhyme goes: "First comes love, then comes marriage …" to which we can now add, "… then comes two idiots wheeling a cappuccino machine in a baby carriage." Security cameras caught two hapless wedding party members trying to do just that, pushing the $1,000 machine along in a pram. One of them went on to further distinguish himself that night by first booting in a hotel window and then attempting to kick out the windshield of a police cruiser.

All told, 12 people were arrested on that special day, including the groom, fathers of the bride and groom, and the best man, whose lack of basic diplomacy skills could be blamed for sparking the fiasco. The newly married man's wedding scrapbook will be a unique specimen, containing, as it could, paperwork related to his charge of "first-degree riot" on his big day.

Here Comes the Blathered Bride

QUEENSLAND NEWS PRESS, SEPTEMBER 2003;

SUNDAY MAIL (U.K.), SEPTEMBER 2003

Getting married involves locking fortunes with someone permanently, or if not permanently, at least until the ink dries on the papers from the quickie Mexican divorce that follows. For most, though, marriage means forsaking all others, even the flirty attractive ones who you tell yourself would definitely be up for it, and settling down to the limitations of monogamy.

As such, it requires some serious consideration, mostly to make absolutely certain that you couldn't have done any better. Once one does decide to tie the proverbial knot, there should be no requirement stating that you need to be sober or clear-headed during the wedding ceremony. After all, you may be overwhelmed at the thought of all the fun you are shutting out of your life in order to enter into this legally binding agreement, and a few cocktails might help lighten your step down the aisle.

A registrar performing the ceremony for a couple from an English seaside town, however, did not see things this way. When the couple showed up to exchange their vows, the registrar said that they were too drunk to fully understand the importance and solemnity of the ceremony, and he refused to proceed.

The pair was sent away to sober up, and the ceremony finally went ahead five hours later.

The bride confessed to having tucked away a few gin and tonics prior to the nuptials. This was her third marriage, she said. Rather than being horrified at the course of events on her special day, she found it entertaining—possibly in contrast to the other, more dignified snooze-fests to which she'd been party. "The whole thing was hilarious," she said. "If it had gone smoothly it would have been boring."

If I Married Her, I Want a Divorce

UNITED PRESS INTERNATIONAL (U.S.), NOVEMBER 1981

Alcohol can undoubtedly help lessen the stress of an important event. Gargling with and swallowing a glass of vodka can, for example, make that personal loan interview a bit more relaxed (if not successful), or make things more social on your children's PTA night.

There is a risk to mellowing out with the help of alcohol though: you may accidentally drink yourself to the point where the important occasion for which you'd been steeling yourself gets blacked out entirely. If the upcoming event is your own wedding, you should perhaps limit yourself to the absolute maximum your body is able to imbibe before it all goes black and you wake up dragging tin cans tied to strings behind your car with no clue as to how they or you got there.

A North Carolina man (we'll call him Edmund in the highly unlikely case that this storied romance took a more positive turn and his grandkids are reading it) filed a claim with an area court requesting that the woman he had been living with for seven years provide proof that they were married.

Edmund claimed that he had taken a trip to South Carolina with his main squeeze while he was in his early twenties. He apparently got so smashed there that when his girlfriend told him after they left that they had gotten hitched, he took her at her word even though he had no recollection of a ceremony.

As time passed, Edmund began to be curious about the supposed wedding and why he could only remember whistling for the next round, and asked his bride to cough up the marriage certificate. She repeatedly refused to produce the document, which led to his taking legal action.

In the proceeding, he also requested that if the two were in fact married, he be granted an immediate divorce.

I Do ... Know I'm Making the Mistake of My Life

Sunday Mail (Australia), December 2004

You need only mention the word *marriage* and you will hear somebody pipe up about the sorry state of the institution, how 50 percent of marriages end in divorce, and how in Hollywood, Glade air fresheners outlast matrimonial promises. The marriage in this story trumps even the shortest of Hollywood unions with its brevity, but while those in Lotus Land are done away with through snappy annulments and the efforts of lawyers in Caribbean countries, some blood was shed before the two in this story were able to make their final split.

The British couple had known each other for only a few months when they decided to take that walk down the aisle together. They invited 50 friends and relatives to witness the ceremony at the local registry office and to attend the reception that followed.

The groom said later that the turning point at the reception came when he toasted the bridesmaids. A witness and a friend of the bride told the *Sunday Mail* a different version, saying that when the groom said he was "toasting the bridesmaids," he was actually "standing on the top table sozzled on gallons of ale shouting at the guests."

Regardless of these differing versions of events, the groom to this day more than likely bears a scar testifying to what happened next. Angered by his drunken antics, the bride took her new hubby outside and clobbered him over the head with a heavy ashtray, leaving a wound that would later take seven stitches to close.

The groom then returned to the reception hall, grabbed a hat stand and hauled it "like a javelin" across the hall and toward the bar, sending barmen scattering to the kitchen—where they called police.

His Olympian heave into the bar was just a warm-up, however. When police arrived and a constable tried to apprehend him, the newlywed head-butted him in the face. Once they hauled him into the police van, he grabbed another officer, put him in a headlock and punched him in the eye.

Some 90 minutes after it began, the couple's wedded life together was over, with both parties saying a honeymoon was out of the question and that they did not want to lay eyes on each other again. "I'm glad to be rid of that woman," the groom told the *Mail.* "My wedding day was a complete nightmare—the biggest mistake of my life—and I'm just glad it's over."

A Boot for the Bootlegger

Women in the Romanian city of Nistoresti forced the closure of a 24-hour booze shop operating in the town by staging protests and filing complaints with consumer protection officials. The women claimed that the store supplied their men with low-grade booze on credit at all hours of the night and that as a result of all that cheap hooch, their men had become impotent and many domestic disputes had arisen. (Ananova.com, U.K., May 2005)

In a Bind

DIE BURGER (GERMANY), FEBRUARY 2006

The saying "Better late than never" does not necessarily apply in the cases of job interviews, airline flights, certain incisions during surgical procedures and especially weddings.

Showing up at a wedding reception after skipping the ceremony is reprehensible. Worse still is showing up right in the middle of the ceremony—so if you do, it's best to commandeer a tray of hors d'oeuvres, loosen that bow-tie a little and hide out in the nearest bathroom until the "I do's" are uttered. There is usually no excuse for being late for *your own* wedding, and in most cases saying "Well, I was tied up" would not fly. Sadly, that is not a euphemism in this case.

A German tattoo shop owner was on an Air Namibia flight from Frankfurt to Cape Town via Windhoek in Namibia for his own wedding, scheduled that afternoon. Getting an early start on the festivities of the day, he proceeded to get madly drunk on board and was seen stealing food from a child's plate (presumably the child was not his own), sniffing a white powder from his hands and generously offering his fellow passengers medication from his backpack. The backpack, when later searched, was found to contain two bottles of vodka, a container with pills, other medicine and, the pièce de résistance, a "homemade cookie in a plastic bag."

Flight attendants tied the blasted man up using the typical restraints used to hold unruly passengers, but he was able to break free. Fearing that he could possibly open the exit door and cause them all to be sucked to an untimely death from on high, flight attendants corralled the ornery drunk and hog-tied him using their own pantyhose.

Perhaps in a tribute to his country's national pastime, the airplane staff gave the German a yellow card—in this case a final warning for ignoring safety issues that will go on a permanent file. After being arrested and paying a fine he arrived, late for his own wedding, in Cape Town.

20

Last Call and Last Rites: Funereal Debauchery

When I die, I want to decompose in a barrel of porter and have it served in all the pubs in Dublin. I wonder would they know it was me?

—J.P. DONLEAVY, *THE GINGER MAN*

Wake the Dead

THE HERALD (U.K.), JULY 1993

For many in the West, a wake represents the last time, in this terrestrial sphere, that one will ever have to be in the room when cousin Edward challenges someone to "try, just try" to open his clenched fist. Wakes are often grey, sombre affairs, where even the drinking is solemn; however, as the wake of a 71-year-old Scottish grandmother demonstrated, holding one in a pub can have unexpected repercussions.

At the wake, one of the recently deceased's boys got into a heated argument with the owner of the public house; the men at the pub started fighting, and when the mourners were ejected into the pub's parking lot, the melee escalated.

When police arrived on the scene they ignored the cardinal rule of bar fights, known to even the most infrequent pub crawler: never underestimate the women. The females in attendance at the wake pounced on and injured three constables and a sergeant with vicious kicks, punches and scratches, and even poured a pint over the head of one of the boys in blue.

Thirty of the woman's relatives and their families were involved in the send-off dust-up and all were reprimanded and fined. The overall tab for the brawl, not counting the pint used to shower a patrolman, came to £1,800.

DISHONOURABLE MENTION
Funeral Disservice

Funerals have been conducted to honour the dead since around 35,000 BC, and while every culture and religion has its own traditions, having a dead-drunk cleric preside over the ceremony is definitely not one of them.

A curate in South Yorkshire resigned after complaints from the bereaved that he had, like a newly lip-pierced kid at the mall, slurred his way through the service. At the request of the family, who noted his unsteady gait as he staggered out of the crematorium, the reverend showed up to look into the matter. Following the curate home, the reverend found him flopped in a chair beside a bottle of sherry.

The reverend later said the curate had "done the honourable thing" and resigned—but apparently he spoke too soon. In an unabashed move, the curate asked the Bishop of Sheffield for his job back, to which the bishop replied, "There is no question of him returning." (*Courier-Mail*, U.K., June 1992; *The Guardian*, U.K., July 1992)

Procession Indiscretion

ASSOCIATED PRESS, JUNE 2005

Drunk driving, also commonly referred to as "How the hell else am I going to get home? Walk?" has fallen quite soundly into society's disfavour after having for years enjoyed a quiet, almost respected place with other now-taboo actions like throwing garbage out of a car window while driving down a country road.

Perhaps the strangest drunk driving case on record, and one that will probably make it into the literature of anti–drunk driving campaigns for years to come, occurred in Missouri, right in the middle of a funeral procession—one held for a man killed by a drunk driver no less.

A local man with a blood-alcohol level of 0.136 percent (state limit: 0.08) plowed through the funeral procession. While it might take a high-powered telescopic lens and the work of some of the larger industrial satellite imaging companies to find a silver lining in this tale, at least the driver was *not* the drunk responsible for the death of the man whose funeral was being held.

Cops, who had been providing an escort for the procession, witnessed the boozed-up driver veer through the crowd before crashing into a pharmacy—a prescription for disaster. Thirty irate and incredulous mourners swarmed the crashed car and began challenging its occupants, while police called in reinforcements and helped to break up what could have been a most thorough shit-kicking.

There is perhaps a special space in the parking garage in the ninth circle of hell for the driver, who was arrested on misdemeanour charges of driving while intoxicated, leaving the scene of an accident, failure to stop at a stop sign, failure to have insurance and (this is actually on the books, leaving one to wonder about the thickness of the book) driving through a funeral procession.

Suburban Sprawl-Out

HERALD SUN (AUSTRALIA), AUGUST 2000

In 1991, between his stints as a feather-boa-wearing, tough-turkey-talking wrestler and governor of the great state of Minnesota, Jesse "The Body" Ventura hosted a game show called *The Grudge Match*. Contestants on the show had some sort of personal grudge with one another—quite frequently they were feuding neighbours—and were made to resolve their dispute in a pro-wrestling-style bout. There was always a strange twist thrown in to make things interesting; for example, they had to wrestle in spaghetti or pudding, or use fire extinguishers and giant foam hammers.

The plug was pulled on this show quicker than the good governor could have taken a foreign object out of his trunks and stuck it in a studio executive's eye. For the time it was on, though, it served a valuable social function: giving people a dispute reso-lution mechanism that did not involve, as in the following story, a gun.

An Australian man and his family had just returned home from a funeral and were in the midst of hosting the wake when their next-door neighbour started up his noisy lawnmower.

Anyone who has tried to enjoy a moment's peaceful contemplation in suburbia only to be vexed by some yahoo with power tools or a lawnmower (this did take place at 6 P.M. after all) will be able to relate to what the man did next. Taking a housemate's air rifle, he went to his upstairs bedroom window and fired off two shots. The gunman and budding Lee Harvey Oswald was hoping that the shots would ricochet off the offending lawnmower operator's boot (which he knew to be steel-toed, his lawyer later said) and somehow jam up the works of the mower.

The shot did hit the man's boot but it did not stop the mowing. A second shot, this one lodging in the man's right shin, did.

After his arrest, the shooter expressed deep remorse, calling the incident a case of "sheer drunken stupidity."

The victim decided his family was not secure living in that house—a logical assumption given the amount of lawnmowing your average homeowner has to attend to—and decided to move.

Tombstone Tippler and Tipper

ANH (U.S.), SEPTEMBER 2005; BELGA NEWS AGENCY (BELGIUM), SEPTEMBER 2005

Bladders being what they are, drinking large volumes over the course of the evening has one inevitable consequence: the need to release that long Niagara Falls–like burst of what is commonly known as a "beer piss." Indeed, as the old saying goes: You can't buy beer, you can only rent it. But what do you do when you're walking home from the bar, there's no bathroom in sight, and nature calls?

Owing to basic physiological differences, a drinking woman with a beer bladder cannot relieve herself in the simple carefree manner enjoyed by her male counterparts. She is forced for the most part to try to ride it out until suitable facilities present themselves, or in the worst-case scenario, to find a place to squat and let go.

There is probably no more deserted place for such an act at nighttime than a cemetery, yet as this cautionary tale shows, it can be a dangerous choice. A 33-year-old Belgian woman was on her way home from a bar when she decided to make a shortcut through a cemetery, where she took advantage of the secluded surroundings to relieve herself.

She crouched between two gravestones and let nature do its work. At some point, though, she stumbled and grabbed on to one of the tombstones to steady herself. The heavy stone came loose and fell on top of her, and in a death strange on many levels, she suffocated.

21
Festive Cheers:
Hooch on the Holidays

Wassail, wassail, all over the town,
Our toast it is white and our ale it is brown
 —"Gloucestershire Wassail," a traditional Christmas carol

Season's Beatings

Daily Mail (U.K.), October 2004

Saint Nicholas (AD 280) is the patron saint of Russia, parish clerks and scholars, but unfortunately his celestial guarding duties do not extend to rioting yobs in Santa suits. Ol' Saint Nick himself was probably doing subterranean cartwheels when a royal rumble involving thousands of Father Christmases broke out in the streets of Newtown, Wales.

Being a saint, ol' Nick would likely find it a further affront that this melee took place at the end of a charity run featuring 4,000 people dressed up in his likeness, or at least the version of his likeness that Coca-Cola popularized about 100 years ago.

The marathon, meant to benefit presumably either the poor or the infirm (reports did not specify), featured the multitude of would-be jolly elves festooned in red felt and fur, sweating it out a few months before Christmas. Alarm bells, and not those of the jingling variety, should have sounded in the minds of event organizers when the decision was made to provide these 4,000 men, who were likely already near dehydration from running in those heavy Santa clothes, with Christmas toddies at the finish line.

Christmas cheer turned to Christmas fear-and-loathing as the Santas proceeded to tie one on and then, worse still, to try to bash one another's heads in. Fortunately, this red-nosed riot was brought to a quick close by police, who added their own chapter to the Santa Claus tradition by clubbing several of the fat men in red suits with batons and pepper-spraying more than one gregarious old elf into yuletide submission.

Mommy, Santa Smells Funny

CHICAGO SUN-TIMES, DECEMBER 1994; ASSOCIATED PRESS, DECEMBER 1994

Mall Santas are a brave lot. They must all contend with the same long days spent under the glare of a shopping mall's neon lights, schmaltzy piped-in Christmas music, and of course an endless procession of snivelling youngsters being brought in to sit on their knees and voice greed rivalled only by that of landholders in feudal times.

With such a working environment, it is perhaps unsurprising that when one looks back on Christmas past one may recall a faint whiff of something other than milk and cookies emanating from under the phoney white beards.

A mall Santa from Southampton, England, was one such old elf. He would ready himself for a day on the job by drinking copious amounts of red wine, because he thought it would give his cheeks that needed rosy glow as well as provide him with the liquid courage needed to be at his jolly best.

Rosy-cheeked as it may have rendered him, the wine also had the natural effect of getting him quite drunk, which comes as little surprise when one considers both the amount he was drinking and also the grade of the alcohol. He claimed to have been drinking red wine, one and a half boxes per day to be exact, all day long between his visits with the tots. Boxed wine, as any ghetto oenologist will tell you, packs a bigger wallop than its bottled cousin.

After one kiddie took leave of the increasingly jolly elf, the man stood up, found that his legs, in the manner of Santa's reindeer, could not be summoned, and dove head first through the department-store window.

Fortunately, the heavily padded Santa suit cushioned his fall and he sustained no injuries. Amazingly, getting falling-down drunk on a day spent mostly in the company of children under the age of 7 did not cost the man his mall gig, thanks to a very forgiving store manager who simply told him to drink less.

Terrible Breath but, Oh, What a Smile!

Scientists have long heralded the salubrious effects of red wine (when it is consumed by the glass, not the box), yet it has long been known to stain your teeth like cigarettes, coffee and other of life's enjoyments. But there's a positive side, say scientists from Laval University in Quebec, who presented a paper for the American Association for Dental Research claiming that polyphenols, a compound in red wine, actually stave off the effect of periodontal diseases affecting the gums. (*Western Mail*, U.K., March 2006)

O, Christmas Tree Surgeon

THE INDEPENDENT (U.K.), DECEMBER 2000

The tradition of the Christmas tree is said to have originated in Germany and from there spread to the rest of the world. German Prince Albert—of "Do you have him in a can? Well, you better let him out!" fame—married Queen Victoria and in 1841 put up the first Christmas tree at Windsor Castle to remind him of his homeland.

Lyrics to the popular yuletide ditty "O, Christmas Tree" vary depending on the source but with lines like "O, Christmas tree, O, Christmas tree / how steadfast are your branches …," it is perhaps a song better enjoyed in its original incomprehensible German.

In many Western countries, the town Christmas tree has become a staple of the season, and in large urban centres such as New York and London its lighting is at least the 38th most important task on every mayor's December to-do list.

In smaller towns, presiding over this special occasion is the domain of celebrities, both small and big *C* alike. No less notable an actress than *Coronation Street*–regular Holly Newman was in attendance to switch on the lights of the 40-foot Christmas tree in Melton Mowbray town in Leicestershire in 2000.

Less than a week later, however, a drunken 25-year-old tree surgeon, egged on by friends and in what one would assume to be a gross violation of professional ethics, felled the fir with a chainsaw. He escaped on foot before police could catch him.

The tree doc was later arrested and ordered to pay for the cost of replacing the tree as well as do 120 hours of community service.

On the Under-Card of Easter Bunny versus Local Favourite

COURTTV.COM, APRIL 2006

In a street altercation, you can typically count on the help of a good Samaritan to jump to your assistance with the following exceptions: you're deafeningly rebuking an 8-year-old who's not the fruit of your loins, or you're engaged in a heated shouting match with an elderly woman in a walker for slipping ahead of you in the grocery express line with one more than "eight items or less" (you've counted).

To add to such a list, which is by no means exhaustive (but if it were it would occupy countless pages, thereby interrupting the leisurely flow of what you see here, not to mention being a mightily boring read), you can definitely add asking Old Saint Nick to put up his holiday dukes.

In Lehigh Acres, Florida, which like many places in the Sunshine State has a name that could grace a retirement home, a man tried to engage in a tussle with the jolly one. A 20-year-old approached

Santa, who was sitting in his convertible (his ride of choice in near tropical climes) at a local fast-food restaurant.

When Santa told the holiday drunk that there were no gifts for him, not even a delightful cognac in a commemorative Christmas box, the drunk began to antagonize the man in red, which soon resulted in fists flying at Father Christmas. The man even attempted to haul the red-robed fellow out of his slick ride. Luckily for Santa, he had two henchmen—in this case, henchwomen—in the car, skilled in the art of hand-to-hand combat, who grabbed the man by the shirt and tossed him aside like a yellow mattress on garbage day.

The attacker was found later with a lump on his face, looking like he had been used as a sparring partner during George Foreman's pre-custom-cookware-glory years, and was promptly arrested by authorities. He conceded that Santa was a lot more powerful than he had anticipated.

'Twas the Night Before Christmas (and Some Drunk Idiot Climbed on the Roof)

CNN, DECEMBER 2003

The words *chimney sweep* conjure up images from Dickensian times, when pickpockets with toothless grins and quips at the ready, epidemic poisonings and freewheeling carnal escapades predating penicillin captured the popular imagination.

Chimney sweeps were often seen as good luck charms, preventing, as they did, the smoking out of Santa as he parachuted down the chute, but this notion didn't sit well with the 12-year-olds whose small size (or slave–boss employment relationship) qualified them to be sent down themselves with a brush in hand while their masters got drunk on cheap gin.

In Minnesota, a man full of Christmas optimism got naked and lowered himself into the chimney of a local bookstore, and while we appreciate this unorthodox devotion to literacy, his getting stuck didn't help matters.

A local police official noted that the man was lucky in that he was stuck there for only a few hours and at a time when the fireplace was not in use—however, the authors still tend to associate being lucky with finding a pair of sunglasses that someone left in a bar, especially if they fit just right.

The man's story was that he had been drinking heavily and had climbed atop the building, whereupon he accidentally dropped his keys down the chute. He surmised that his stripping down would better allow him to fit into the 12-by-12-inch opening.

It didn't, and he was rescued by sledgehammer-wielding fire-fighters, then arrested for attempted robbery, thus putting a damper on his December 25th. As an official noted, "He doesn't appear to be a hard-core criminal, just stupid."

Pass Around the *Akvavit*!

A popular Norwegian drink, particularly around the Christmas holidays, *akvavit* is widely believed to help in the digestion of rich foods and is served during the appetizer course of meals along with pickled herring, crayfish, lutefisk or smoked fish. A common quip has it that the fine spirit helps the fish find their way down to the stomach. (Wikipedia.com)

The Snowshoer Who Went Up a Mountain
and Got Too Drunk to Come Down

ASSOCIATED PRESS, JANUARY 2000

The 1993 movie *Alive,* the working title of which is rumoured to have been *Eating Ass,* chronicled the true-life story of a group of people who survived a plane crash in the Andes Mountains and the subsequent cannibalism that brought the lot of them closer together. But not everyone who gets stranded on a mountain has to resort to sticking a fork in his best friend's thigh before being rescued, as this story shows.

A Colorado man was one of three hardy souls who decided to avoid the madding crowd and spend New Year's Eve of the new millennium in a remote cabin on Smuggler Mountain.

When the mountain partier dawdled the following morning before heading back down, it was agreed that he would catch up with his two companions later in the day at the trailhead.

While his friends went ahead, the man, apparently in no great hurry to return to civilization, proceeded to dip into the remaining booze in the cabin. By the time he eventually did decide to make the descent, he was completely blasted, and, to add a further layer of peril, a vicious snowstorm was kicking up.

Fortunately, he was intercepted on the trail by the group on its way up that had booked the cabin for that night. Meeting him staggering down the trail, they talked him into returning to the cabin and waiting for assistance.

His pals had by then alerted the authorities about their missing friend and Mountain Rescue Aspen dispatched a dozen members to search for him in the storm. They eventually found him sobering up in the Smuggler Mountain cabin and hauled him to safety on the back of a snowmobile.

A county sheriff's deputy reckoned that had it not been for his meeting the group on the way down, the New Year's reveller could have gone the way of so many other adventurers. If expedition lore is to be taken at face value, this would mean dying of exposure and becoming mountain fodder for horrified schoolchildren to find frozen some 30 years later.

Let the Drinking Games Begin
NATIONAL POST (CANADA), JANUARY 2001

Citius, Altius, Fortius—or Swifter, Higher, Stronger—is the official motto of the Olympic Games, which, come to think of it, reads much better than Corrupt, Illegitimate and Underhanded, especially in Latin. In Whistler, B.C., where the 2010 Winter Games are to be held, digging deep for that one last surge to the finish refers more to that queasy point in the evening when the cheap lager being funnelled by the keg is mercifully running out and the phrase "what goes down, must come up" is being played out in chalet bathrooms.

The Royal Canadian Mounted Police, or the Mounties—made all the more famous by Epcot—called the 2000 New Year's festivities in Whistler a "near riot plagued by drunk and violent behaviour," as 80 extra officers had to be brought in to calm things down.

As is often the case after the countdown and off-key warbling of "Auld Lang Syne," some party-goers ushered in the New Year by hurling chunks of ice and bottles at one another, as well as hurling for real.

One woman was taken to hospital after a man, drunk as a mule, in an aerial tribute to *lucha libre* Mexican wrestling, leapt off a bar table and landed on her.

But a 16-year-old attendee from Vancouver, apparently getting a head start on his adult drinking years, called the police "picky and finicky," saying that they went overboard in rounding up the revellers.

All told, more than 100 people were sent to the drunk-tank, which was equipped to handle only your average weekend's worth of après-skiers tossed from chalets. The drunken overflow had to be moved to a separate facility.

Many people in the area began to call for "dry" festivities in future. (Since when has *dry,* apart from referring to wit, had positive connotations? But we digress.)

An organizer for New Year's celebrations in Whistler said she believed that celebrations that year were *more* peaceful and *less* rowdy than the previous year. A local bar owner chimed in that the police seemed to want Whistler "to be like Vatican Square, not like the village square."

Millennium Bonkers

THE PEOPLE (U.K.), JANUARY 2000

The buildup to the changing of the millennium in 2000 was marked by hysterical people predicting all manner of world-altering developments to coincide with the historic milestone—the Y2K bug shutting off the Internet porn pipeline, natural catastrophes, political upheavals, the physiology of humankind changing so that we would sprout gills and be able to breathe under water (well, this point of view was confined to frequenters of a few select drinking establishments; nonetheless it *was* voiced, if memory serves).

What did take place was pretty much what takes place any other New Year's, with the exception of this one being met with much more anxiety, and bigger and better booze-filled parties. Grand celebrations were staged all over the world, and in Britain the top shindig was undoubtedly that held at the Millennium Dome, where even Prime Minister Tony Blair and his wife were to be found publicly kissing at the tolling of the midnight bell, and Her Majesty and Prince Philip enjoyed New Year's libations.

Minutes after these eminences had piled into their limos and called it a night, and an hour past last call, the cleanup crew came upon a "good-looking couple" in their twenties—one wonders if the response would have been different if, say, the offending couple had been uglier than the paired arses of two cows—welcoming the next thousand years with a very drunken and public shag.

To top it off, the pair were sharing this special moment in an area of the Millennium Dome called "The Shared Ground Zone." As one Dome worker was quoted as saying, "The ground wasn't all they were sharing." Another wag working there went on to observe that in the area that aimed to "explore real and imaginary communities from around the U.K.," the pair "had obviously been doing an awful lot of exploring."

Though the staff found the occasion a cause for mirth, the "Millennium Bonkers," as the popular Sunday tabloid *The People* dubbed them, were anxious to leave the scene of their amorous merrymaking. Red-faced, they gladly accepted a ride home from Dome staff.

VIII

Distinction Under the Influence: Giving Remarkable Drunks the Recognition They Deserve

The title of this section could conceivably apply to every story in this book. After all, it is a fact for which we can all be thankful that the stories here are the exception rather than the norm. Who among us would actually want to attend a public event with these people or have one of them pull up next door with a moving van?

The blue-ribbon boozehounds of this section, however, go that extra mile and they all have one thing in common: they put absolutely zero forethought into their behaviour—not only throwing caution to the wind, but hoisting the mainsails of stupidity on the good ship Senseless. These are stories that you read in the morning newspaper and, when you're confident that the featured party is not a close relative or dating your daughter, you shake your head and utter a laugh that is not without some pity.

Alcohol alone cannot justify the behaviour of those featured in The Thinkers. Call it what you will—a genetic flaw, or the result of being dropped on one's head at an early age—but there's something else at play when someone does something like putting a key part of his anatomy at peril in a mousetrap, for the second time no less, or getting himself arrested on a drunkenness-related charge for the second time in as many hours.

The lights do not get much brighter in Drunken Dares and Derring-Do. Here we see what happens when a person works up the drunken moxie to accept a dare or a bet or attempt a stunt that they would never consider in their sober hours. The results speak for themselves, and include a man nearly meeting his maker under fast-flying hooves and a guy who now has to go by an incredibly ridiculous new name.

Although getting a jag on can get you into trouble, fortune occasionally does seem to smile on the soused. In the interests of fairness, we've chronicled cases where being drunk, it could be argued, saved the lives of the people in question.

Why is it that a fall from a height that would kill your average man did not kill some of the drunkards in these stories? We will avoid any sort of mystical speculation, but suffice to say that such incidents are rare and we advise you to think twice before getting up on a shaky patio chair on your 40th-storey balcony with a bellyful of Bacardi. The odds are not in your favour.

22

The Thinkers: Stupid Human Tricks

There is nothing worse than aggressive stupidity.

—JOHANN WOLFGANG VON GOETHE

Of Mousetraps and Morons

THE SUN (U.K.), JANUARY 2006

A zipper pulled up in haste, as most men will attest, can bring about obscenity-inducing pain that will make you forever after consider wearing nothing but sweatpants. Zippers are not the greatest threat, though, for man and his very best friend—the greatest threat of all is the diminished capacity for critical thinking that can cause someone to make a stupid decision while drunker than a fart.

A pub manager was entertaining a drunken group of his friends with the story of how, at the age of 14 in a "schoolboy prank" (we're assuming an all-boys' school, because this sort of "prank" seems par for the course in such places), he got his privates caught in a mouse-trap. He required (prepare your face, dear reader, for a grimace) a total of 14 stitches.

That he would choose to recount this tale in any place other than on his therapist's couch is difficult enough to fathom, but what happened next truly sets him apart.

One of his friends asked him to explain in detail what had happened during the incident and even produced a mousetrap as a visual aid. The pub manager set the trap up on a pool table, unzipped himself, walked toward the trap and, liquored up as he was, lost his footing and fell—snapping up his goods for a second time.

"I must be the only bloke in Britain to have caught my bits in a mousetrap not once but twice," he said later, and one can only hope that is true.

His second entanglement with the mousetrap was not as serious as his first, thank goodness, as he only "nipped the end of [his] privates"—though he had to receive a tetanus injection. The nurses at the hospital, he said, found the incident, particularly because it was a recurrence, "hilarious."

Drying Out

REUTERS, NOVEMBER 2005

According to our "research"—which, unlike uncovering the puzzle of the human genome or unlocking the mystery as to why the woolly mammoth no longer lumbers along beside us, only involved plunking terms into Google—*three sheets to the wind* is a nautical term. Google says it was used famously by "Chucky" Dickens in *Dombey and Son*. It actually refers to the ropes that hold the sails in place; when they're too loose, the vessel lurches about like a drunken sailor (see Sloshed at Sea for clear examples of this).

On most days one likely would have wanted to hold the sheets of a 60-year-old German man to a very strong wind, for he was in the habit of urinating in his bed rather than getting up to relieve himself. Well, habit or not, that did happen on at least one occasion when he capped off a night on the piss by having one, all over his mattress and bedding.

What was worse than the man's sloth in committing this act in the first place (it's like your granny always told you—if you're old enough to go to the bar, you're old enough to go to the damn loo) was the method he chose to dry the soiled mattress the next morning. According to a police official, the mercifully unnamed man switched on a hairdryer, placed it on the bed and left his apartment.

Now, not surprisingly, urine and electricity don't mix. And mattresses, as any fear-mongering one-hour consumer-alert program will tell you, are typically made using highly flammable material.

Thus the man returned to his apartment later in the day to find it, and all of his belongings, in flames.

DISHONOURABLE MENTION
Hammered at the Hearing

If you take to the hooch like a pooch to a favourite pair of slippers and that love has gotten you in some legal trouble, it is in your best interest to prove to a judge that you are committed to turning over a new leaf. Under no circumstances, though, should you get a jag on before your court appearance.

In Pennsylvania, a defendant who showed up to face the music for a car wreck resulting from drunk driving was marching to the unsteady beat of his own drum when he admitted to the judge that he had had just a "couple of beers" prior to the hearing.

The judge, not buying the man's accounting, challenged him to submit to a blood-alcohol test to prove it. The defendant promptly failed, and admitted sheepishly that he had actually had six. (Associated Press, October 1998)

Chugging Lugs

NEWS24.COM (SOUTH AFRICA), NOVEMBER 2005

Games that employ observation, intellect or memory are often beyond the scope of the hardened drinker, as evidenced by the slobbering drunk at the end of the bar blurting out poorly thought-through retorts on pub-trivia night and scoring in the negative integers. Not surprisingly, drinking games tend to be based on either speed or quantities and are much more in keeping with the muddled attention span of those involved.

In game theory, tennis or boxing, for example, are zero-sum games because one person's gain is another's loss and it is impossible for both players to win (or lose). In drinking games, this is more complex because typically the "winners" are often the biggest losers.

Such was the case in Tanzania, where a man participated in an unsanctioned drinking contest in a bar in the country's capital— "unsanctioned" in this case likely referring to the notable absence of an attending physician.

The man, identified in news reports only as "Shame," although this might have been an editorial comment that was somehow lost in translation, wolfed down a staggering quart of vodka en route to his Churchillian "victory at all costs" in the illustrious contest.

Ever the showman, Shame washed the vodka down with two bottles of beer, after which he had to be rushed to the hospital to have his stomach pumped.

Sadly, he didn't make it, and is now, somewhere, food for worms.

His closest competitor, the appropriately handled "Johnny Walker," was admitted to hospital but survived. The third competitor—the actual winner, in retrospect, at least in relative terms—had earlier declared himself vanquished, and staggered home even before his colleagues lost consciousness.

High-Powered Hooch

No word if drinking contests were ever held using this creation, but our guess is that if so, the event would indeed have been a short one, especially if conducted within 10 feet of an open flame. According to the *Guinness Book of World Records,* the strongest commercially available alcoholic drink dates from the first half of the 20th century, when the Estonian Liquor Monopoly marketed a beverage that was distilled from potatoes. It was 196-proof (98 percent alcohol).

Dishonourable Mention

Heavy Yolk to Bear

From devilled to poached, Benedict to omelette, soufflé to quiche, there are thousands of ways to cook eggs—but only four if you're a greasy-spoon hash-slinger or budding summer-camp cordon bleu frying them into oily submission to ward off salmonella-related litigation.

Egg cartons, however, though they may be a desirable adjunct to finger-painting for preschool arts and crafts, are rarely called for to add a hint of flavour or texture to your morning *huevos*.

Nevertheless, firefighters in Norway were called after a fledgling fusion chef, famished following a boozy night on the town, was trying to fry some eggs he had forgotten to take out of their carton. The impromptu recipe, which may or may not have called for lightly pan-seared cardboard, caused a minor grease fire. (*The Press*, New Zealand, February 2003)

The Unhappy Medium

WAKEFIELD TODAY (U.K.), MARCH 2006; *YORKSHIRE POST TODAY*, MARCH 2006

The following involves a protagonist who's distinguished himself such that his inclusion in The Thinkers is not an ironic slight. A Yorkshire-born medium described as "the most accurate in Britain" (which is akin to being "the world's tallest dwarf")—who, like other purported psychics, doesn't use his "gifts" for any practical purpose whatsoever, such as predicting lottery numbers, playing the stock market or getting involved in real estate—had his routine interrupted by a voice of reason, admittedly a slurred one, from the crowd.

The heckler, not exactly guided by the Socratic dialectic, shouted obscenities during the show, undermining the sanctity of the proceedings. As the psychic told a tearful woman that the 31st of October was an important anniversary for her and her husband, the heckler shouted "Halloween!" which prompted a cuff from the miffed medium that it's safe to say nobody in attendance could've predicted.

The pugilist prognosticator said that there were people in the crowd who had received otherworldly communication from loved ones that were not of the text-message variety, and that the interrupter had spoiled it for everybody.

The heckler had repeatedly gone to and from the bar and had berated the clairvoyant during the show, said berating culminating in their confrontation. The medium claimed that this was the first time he had ever been heckled, and we have to assume that unlike his prognostications, this statement had a basis in truth.

Look, Kids, Grandpa's in the Guinness Book of World Records!

Brisbane man Tommy Johns gets a mention in the *Guinness Book of World Records* for having been convicted of drunkenness 200 times.

When Irish Guys Are Silent

THE IRISH TIMES, APRIL 1995

The cheesy quip goes like this: "A good friend helps you move. A great friend helps you move a body." In a similar vein, the conduct of two men, undoubtedly best of pals, was questioned in a Dublin inquest that heard that one man drove his drinking buddy around not realizing he was belly-up in the back seat.

The men went on a drinking spree the wildness of which truly beggars belief, knocking back a liver-pickling 5 1/4–gallon drum of home-brewed beer, with one of the men downing 14 pints and the other 20. Rather than calling it a night following that truly heroic feat of drinking, they chased it all down with an additional 10 pints at a pub and, no, they weren't finished yet, a half-bottle of vodka. The comparably more moderate of the two—that is, the one who had opted earlier for 14 rather than 20 pints—decided he would have only a few mouthfuls of vodka before heading off to bed.

Remarkably, that same man, who must have a constitution that is the stuff of railway mythology, was upright and functional the following morning and set about running his errands for the day. Discovering his buddy slumped over in the back seat of the car, he made the assumption that he was sleeping off his incredible toot from the night before, and, knowing that his friend was not the most pleasant sort when woken up after a big night, he carried on first to the Dublin District Court and then to the local pub, where he had scheduled appointments.

At about midday, when he had finished at the local pub, the man finally decided to enlist the help of another friend in rousing the slumbering party in his back seat—only to shake him and find that he was stone dead.

Latvian Unorthodox

The *Guinness Book of World Records,* likely not wanting to encourage a grossly unhealthy image of alcohol-related products, does not include an entry for "world's most iron-gutted drunkard," but if it did the distinction would surely go to a man in Latvia who captured the unofficial record after drinking twice the amount of alcohol normally considered fatal.

The man was found passed out drunk at a bus stop and brought to a hospital, where a test revealed that his blood contained 7.22 parts per million of alcohol. A level of 1.2 is enough for most people to revisit their breakfasts, 3.0 would knock most people out, and 4.0 is considered enough to kill your average mere mortal. The man in question achieved this extraordinary feat of drinking by knocking back a bottle of homemade white lightning. (BBC, December 2003; Reuters, December 2003)

24-Hour Potty People

The Advertiser (Australia), August 1997

Thriftiness, or as some would term it, being a stingy bugger, can take many forms: dropping a quarter in a church collection plate and filching out a nickel's change; cutting open a tube of toothpaste and scraping your brush along the innards before it goes into the garbage; buying a used air-mattress that is heavily discounted because it has a hole, but reckoning that all you really need is a comfortable hour to get to sleep and if it's deflated by the time you wake up, then so what.

There are some times, though, when one needs to open one's wallet and let the moths fly out of it, such as when one needs a public pay toilet. The nominal fee demanded by these would seemingly present an obstacle only to the truly tight-fisted among us.

Six liquored-up teenage girls in a small port town in northeast England, however, found the fee too exorbitant and, drunk and en masse, they squeezed into one single portable toilet to avoid each having to spend 50 p to pee.

The pressure of their combined mass jammed the door lock, so they were stuck in there together for hours. And a portable toilet, as anybody who has ever used one or has had to clean one will tell you, is not the kind of place you want to dally in. The girls pounded on the walls of the toilet and shouted for help for what must have seemed an eternity before one passerby finally heard their plaintive wails and called emergency services.

Firemen took an additional three hours to cut off the top of the crapper using Jaws of Life–type equipment usually reserved for car crashes.

Getting Away with It (Literally)

WGRZ TV Buffalo, February 2006

The Buffalo Bills set a National Football League record for appearing in four consecutive Super Bowl games, all of which they lost. A fellow loser and Buffalo resident, in an effort to buck the decrepit rust-belt city's losing ways, must've had Lady Luck reclining comfortably in the passenger seat when he set a record of his own.

It was about 4 A.M. when Lackawanna cops noticed a vehicle engaged in the "reach for the Gravol, I'm gonna blow biscuits" school of offensive driving, at which point they decided to pull him over. Seeing the man's glassy eyes and smelling alcohol on his breath, they wanted him to take a Breathalyzer test.

After initially declining, the suspect did one better than his home NFL team, failing a mere three of the four Breathalyzer tests administered. Despite the fact that he was then arrested for a DUI while driving with a suspended licence, the man was co-operative with police, so they released him with a ticket specifying his court date and said they would not tow his car, though they did hold on to it.

Cops advised the suspect to have someone come pick him up, and a while later, someone arrived with a spare set of keys. He handed them over to the car's owner, who proceeded to burn rubber out of the parking lot at about 100 miles per hour.

The same officers pulled the motorist over once again, and he was subsequently arrested for a second time on DUI charges—but this time his car was towed to the impound lot for good measure.

The district attorney called the man's ability to nab two DUI arrests in three hours a "hall of shame record." The DA noted, however, that while in most cases the man's second DUI arrest would have been treated as a felony, he managed to avoid that more serious charge because at the time of commission, he had not yet been convicted of the earlier offence.

DISHONOURABLE MENTION
The DUI Relay Team

In The Hague, three DUI charges were racked up in just a few hours and using one vehicle, though in this case it took three perps to do the job.

It began when a 40-year-old man was stopped during a routine traffic check and failed a Breathalyzer test. While a police officer was fining him, a passenger in the man's car grabbed the baton by jumping behind the wheel and speeding off. He was later nabbed by The Hague's crack squad of traffic police, fined and released.

We can only speculate as to what was going through the minds of police when they saw the same vehicle speed past them, this time with a third driver. The drunken relay run ended there with the car being impounded, because the final driver was operating it without a licence. (Agence France-Presse, March 2006)

For Your Eyes Only?

COURIER-MAIL (AUSTRALIA), MARCH 2000; THE SUN (U.K.), MARCH 2000

James Bond, an M16 spy, is frequently featured spending much of his time playing baccarat with beautiful, heavily accented femme fatales in international casinos, bedding them and drinking so much that he could be branded an alcoholic. He, however, would never do anything *this* irresponsible.

A fellow, less fictional, British M16 spy, a man "with a licence to kill time," became the subject of major embarrassment to the British spying outfit when he lost a laptop containing sensitive documents after a drunken night out at a London bar.

Reports speculate that the spy either had the laptop stolen at a London tube station or that he forgot it in a taxi. Regardless, sensing disaster, the M16 agency took out an ad which read: "Academic urgently seeks information leading to the recovery of PhD vital research notes stored on Toshiba 4000 Series CDS laptop computer in black carrying case lost in London on evening 3 March." This wording was chosen as opposed to, say, "Laptop containing sensitive documents vital to national security and the health of the nation lost while owner drunk. Reward for further information."

The laptop was in fact recovered by police about two weeks later. The Foreign Office assured the public, which had been whipped into a frenzy when news of the missing laptop broke four days after the incident, that state security had not been compromised by its loss.

Of course, that is what they *want* you to think. Another report from *The Sun* speculated that the laptop may have contained the names of spies working overseas and could have been connected to the arrest of an M16 spy abroad that occurred shortly before the laptop was retrieved.

United Kingdom Tops in Seeing the Bottom of Pint Glasses

The United Kingdom bested its European neighbours in terms of the amount the average person puts back on a drunken night out. The survey by market analysis firm Datamonitor showed that on average people there down 6.3 units on a night out, the equivalent of 2.2 pints of lager. On average, the European drinking rate indicated by the survey was 5.1 units or around 1.8 pints. Germany finished second in the survey with 5.5 units or 1.9 pints of lager, followed by Spain, France and Italy. (*Daily Mail,* U.K., April 2006)

23
Lucky Drunks

Fortune knocks at every man's door once in a life, but in a good many cases the man is in a neighbouring saloon and does not hear her.

—MARK TWAIN

You Can't Keep a Good Man Down

TORONTO STAR, SEPTEMBER 1990

Plummeting from a high place is probably one of the most exciting ways to bite the biscuit. Indeed, who among us hasn't entertained the notion of the thrilling rush such a jump would elicit and what fleeting images would pass through our minds before we made contact with the pavement below—perhaps the cherished face of a loved one or, if we are less lucky, the theme song to *Three's Company* that we can't seem to get out of our heads.

As an Edmonton, Alberta, man fell from his 20th-storey balcony, the only thing he'd had on his mind, he said later, was the certainty of his own demise.

The man was drunk when he decided to go out to his balcony and adjust a satellite TV wire that was giving him trouble. While standing on a wobbly patio chair, he lost his balance and fell over the railing. He survived the fall by grabbing, on his way down, cable television wires running alongside of the apartment building— cable in effect saving the man's life, despite the disloyalty he had displayed by switching to satellite TV.

To what does he attribute this quick thinking and show of good reflexes? Being pissed. He claims that because he was drunk his adrenalin was pumping and that's what saved his life.

Though grabbing the cables slowed his descent, he still hit the ground hard and broke his back, left heel and three ribs. As he approached "terminal velocity" (which, luckily for him, wasn't terminal), a deceased or living physicist would tell you that his plummeting mass increased the amount of air resistance, which resulted in his pants ripping. He later told reporters that the most painful part of the entire episode was losing the $400 that had been in his pocket.

The accident confined the man to a wheelchair for a period of time as he rehabbed his back, but alas, his motivation for getting out of the chair may not inspire a made-for-TV movie. The band Judas Priest had a gig scheduled at the Edmonton Coliseum the following month, he said, "and that's not music you can sit down to."

Let Me Tell You (What I Remember) about the Hurricane

DAILY TELEGRAPH (AUSTRALIA), SEPTEMBER 2005;

SYDNEY MORNING HERALD, SEPTEMBER 2005

Hurricane Katrina will go down as either the fourth of fifth worst disaster in U.S. history, killing well over 1,000 people and ravaging the coastlines of the Gulf states. New Orleans itself was hard hit by the disaster, but while many were forced to face the full wrath of the hurricane and its aftermath, one visiting Australian was able to avoid the entire episode, his life perhaps saved when he was arrested for drunk and disorderly behaviour and thrown into jail.

The tourist was whooping it up in the best debauched Big Easy style on Bourbon Street in the town's famed party district the night before the hurricane struck. The Aussie apparently became a little too boisterous in his celebrating and was arrested on the D-and-D charge and thrown into New Orleans Parrish Prison.

The next day the hurricane hit, the prison flooded and the prisoners began to riot, forcing officials to transfer all of them to a different facility. During the riot, however, one of the prisoners broke into the property section of the prison and stole the tourist's wallet and credit card.

His parents back in Australia, upon hearing the news of the hurricane and seeing that their son's credit card was being used in the area, but knowing that he had not contacted anyone to let them know he was all right, figured him for dead. They flew to Houston to look for their missing son among the 18,000 homeless New Orleans evacuees being housed there, while various officials continued to search for him.

Eventually an Australian federal police officer got a break in the case, discovering that the man was in a Baton Rouge prison. The inmate's dad, while feeling "over the moon" at the news that his son was okay, nonetheless said that he would have a few choice words about his boy getting locked up in a drunk-tank while on holiday.

Bouncing Right Back Up

ONLYPUNJAB.COM, JANUARY 2005

The ancient Italian astronomer Galileo, for all you readers whose foreheads aren't sloped, theorized that all objects fall at the same rate, after a famous experiment in which he, much to the chagrin of Pisa residents, hurled various objects off their tower and quantified the results. This experiment was to be repeated years later by David Letterman in New York City using watermelons and bowling balls dropped into bathtubs, which garnered similar results.

A lathered Russian man also obeyed the law of uniformly accelerated motion when he lost his balance while on a 40-foot-high balcony and plunged to earth. Not only did "Oleg" survive the fall, he just as extraordinarily survived having quaffed a litre of vodka beforehand. (For those of you playing along at home, and this is by no means advisable without a highly regarded hospital emergency department nearby, a litre is 22 1/2 shots.)

While drinking the vodka at his friend's flat, Oleg began to feel ill and told the assembled he was going out on the balcony for some fresh air—which he did indeed get on his way to the ground. Friends who had witnessed the fall of Oleg figured him for a goner and were shocked to see him stand up, walk back to the apartment and, as anyone would do after having a near-death experience, begin living life to its fullest by returning to his vodka.

Paramedics called to the scene posited that Oleg "must have drunk so much that his muscles and limbs were so relaxed they were almost like jelly, and he bounced off the ground when he hit it like a ball."

The Yellow Road to Freedom

ANANOVA.COM (U.K.), JANUARY 2005; *THE SUN* (U.K.), JANUARY 2005;
THE REGISTER (U.K.), JANUARY 2005; *THE AUSTRALIAN,* JANUARY 2005

Getting drunk in a wintry clime can be something of a bummer, what with the increased risk of dying of exposure that results from lowering your body temperature with alcohol. Winter does have its advantages, though. Chucking snowballs at your friends or at passing cars is great for a laugh, and possibly one of the most enjoyable aspects of a winter wonderland is relieving yourself by using a virgin snowbank as a blank canvas.

Depending on how much you have quaffed over the course of the night you can spell out your initials, Valentine's Day wishes to the special someone in your life or the entire lyrics to your country's national anthem.

A Slovakian resident proved that pissing in the snow can also save your life. He was driving around in his Audi in Slovakia's Tatra Mountains when an avalanche erupted. This was bad news, as anyone who has ever seen a film in which a caveman returns to life after being frozen for thousands of years ago will know.

The trapped motorist opened the window of his buried Audi and attempted to dig himself out with his hands, but soon realized that the car was filling up with snow quicker than he could work. Faced with the grim ramifications, he did what most of us would do in such a situation: cracked open a beer and gave it all some thought.

Eventually nature called, and when it did, the man, who of course was much calmer by this point, fashioned a strategy. He would melt the snow slowly but surely using his own urine. To help him in this great escape were the 60 half-litre bottles of beer he had brought along. That he was alone in the car and expecting to drink that much beer while on holiday is not to be subject to judgment.

A rescue crew found the motorist four days after the avalanche, completely drunk and staggering along a mountain path after having freed himself from the trapped Audi. Drinking all that beer, enough to free himself from the avalanche, was difficult, he said, and as a result his "kidneys and liver hurt." Still, he was glad the cache of beer had proved to be a lifesaver.

Pipeline to the Gods

There are some substances you don't want to see when you turn on the taps in your kitchen sink—like blood, for instance (you'd know you were in the midst of a risible horror film). One Norwegian woman, however, turned on her taps to the kind of discovery that would be every barfly's fantasy: free-flowing beer.

The woman had been doing some washing, she said, when she turned on the taps and thought she was "in heaven." This joyous development was the result of someone working on the pipes in a bar two floors below. He had mistakenly connected a new barrel of beer to a water pipe leading to her flat. The bar got the worst end of things, with water in its beer taps. (Reuters, March 2006)

Legend of the Fall

KARE 11 TV MINNEAPOLIS–ST PAUL, APRIL 2006;
WKOW 27 TV WISCONSIN, APRIL 2006

Taking a flying leap off a balcony is a common Spring Break frat-house stunt, all the more successful if there's a swimming pool below. In such an exploit, you have a few seconds of free fall to try to recall whether said pool actually has a deep end, to see your life pass before your eyes, or more commonly, to holler something ridiculous like "Geronimo!"

As your cannonball is met with wild applause (when in actuality it's your trunks slipping off that is delighting the boozy assembled), you just thank your lucky stars you made it, regroup and rethink that fraternity pledge—and concomitant hazing ritual.

In Wisconsin, a man whose flying leap did *not* end in a swimming pool was lucky to live to see another beer.

While on a drinking binge that involved hitting more bars than a tin cup summoning a jail guard, the man stumbled around in a parking garage, decided he was on the first storey rather than the fourth, and took a flying leap over the guardrail, plunging 44 feet. He was rescued by a firefighter who happened by.

Hospital officials treated the man, believing the wounds he sustained were the result of a vicious beating or a severe car crash. It wasn't until a parking-lot security video was released that emergency room staff determined what had actually taken place.

The victim acknowledged he was just looking for his car at 2:30 A.M.—which still doesn't explain his leap of faith.

DISHONOURABLE MENTION
No Barfly Will Be Left Behind

Being a pub owner is similar in many respects to being a babysitter; very often one has to deal with drooling, incoherent people who are not close relations, face unpleasant bathroom-related incidents and, if something goes awry and injury or worse takes place, bear responsibility.

The manager of a pub in Vermont found this out the hard way when he faced losing his liquor licence for a week after accidentally locking one of his patrons in the bar at closing time, the drinker's-dream equivalent to a child being locked in a toy store overnight.

At around closing time the bar's door fell off its hinges. The manager put the door back in place with the help of other patrons and locked up for the night. Forgotten in the hubbub surrounding the door was a patron who had fallen asleep under a table-soccer game.

He was released the following morning by police after setting off the bar's alarm. (*Daily Telegraph,* Australia, October 2001)

24

Drunken Dares and Derring-Do: Saluting the Wasted Wagerer

Always do sober what you said you'd do drunk. That will teach you to keep your mouth shut.

—ERNEST HEMINGWAY

It's "Drunken Idiot" by a Nose!

THE SCOTSMAN, JUNE 1994

Horses once served man as the primary mode of transport in times of war and at home, but with the advent of the automobile this role became almost completely symbolic. The beasts were then thanked for their years of service with new posts in society as fodder for glue and rendering plants and as a key ingredient in the nation's best dog food.

Another increasingly popular use for horses has been to gather them at racetracks, put little men on top of them, and force them to race with one another while the audience members bring ruination upon themselves through gambling, softening the blow of every lost dollar with a fortifying drink.

Occasionally this bawdy spectacle of gambling, cursing and haggling with hookers is undertaken with pretension. Such is the case when the Royal Family, long accustomed to frivolous horseplay, celebrates in the nearly 300-year-old tradition that is the Royal Ascot, the world's most famous horse race that isn't the Kentucky Derby.

It was at the 1994 running of the Royal Ascot that a 21-year-old man, several furlongs into his own drinking derby, was nearly killed when he ran in front of a galloping racehorse just yards away from the Queen's box.

When asked why he had decided to attempt this drunken finish at the Ribblesdale Stakes, he said he was trying "to get a better look at the 'gorgeous' [source newspaper's quotation marks] women in the Royal Enclosure." He later admitted that his judgment in this regard was helped along by an afternoon spent guzzling lager and rum with his mates. The larrikin said later that he had thought the horses had already passed, but his miscalculation resulted in his being treated to an unwelcome close-up of the underbelly of Papago, the thoroughbred that trampled him.

The Queen, the Queen Mother, the Duke of Edinburgh and Princess Margaret themselves got a close-up view of the drunken commoner almost meeting his end.

Luckily the man suffered only minor head injuries, and the wee jockey was reported to have escaped harm.

The Kentucky Derby Is Decadent

The mint julep has been the drink of choice at the Kentucky Derby for decades—at least among the seats sold to people who aren't gulping back bourbon sans mint. Woodford Reserve, the distillery that makes the famous drinks for the Derby, recently announced plans to appeal to the cream of the crop among the julep-drinking set.

At the 2006 Kentucky Derby, prior to seeing their hard-earned money trod under the hooves of the thoroughbreds on the track, punters were able to dispatch with a fair bit of it to purchase a $1,000 "ultimate" mint julep. Customers who coughed up the cash for this princely grog were able to see the Woodford Reserve's head distiller mix it himself. The julep contained mint from Morocco, ice from the Arctic Circle and sugar from the South Pacific, and was served in a gold-plated cup with a silver straw.

The juleps were not strictly a cash-grab to take advantage of punters at the track; proceeds from their sale went to the Thoroughbred Retirement Foundation, which keeps former race-horses from being sold for slaughter. (Associated Press, April 2006)

Locked Cock and Two Choking Perils

BOSTON HERALD, AUGUST 2005

During Victorian times, female chastity belts were designed to thwart unwanted sexual encounters (such as the kind that might today involve the man in this story). Call it loosening sexual mores, a testament to ever-increasing rights and freedoms, or possibly advances in hacksaw technology, but chastity belts have been out of common circulation for some 200-plus years. Yet a New Hampshire man did, for a couple of weeks, suffer with the modern-day equivalent of a chastity belt, the result of a night spent drinking and a prank played on him by a friend of the type that leaves one not needing enemies.

The incident began when two guys got drunk together, one of them fell asleep and the other proceeded to put a padlock on his slumbering friend's family jewels. Not only was the victim's name not released, but on a sourer note, neither were his testicles—for two weeks, because the victim of this stunt broke the key off in the lock.

Presumably too reticent to approach a Home Depot floor rep for assistance, the 39-year-old victim then tried unsuccessfully to remove the lock himself using a hacksaw and, one would assume, some pretty cautious sawing.

Drunk once again and frustrated at the state of the union below his belt, the man finally broke down, phoned police and told them the entire tale. They arrived at 3:40 A.M. that morning to find him quite drunk and the lock still firmly in place. The officer who responded to the call said later that in his entire 13-year career he had never "seen anything like this."

The man was brought to a nearby hospital and a (no doubt perplexed) locksmith was summoned. A transcript of that call was not saved for posterity, much to the chagrin of the authors. After what was likely a grimace-inducing procedure for all males present, the man and his nether-dwelling friends were reunited "without lasting injury."

Pissed to the Gills

BBC NEWS, JUNE 2003; *THE ARGUS* (U.K.), JUNE 2003;
REUTERS, JUNE 2003; *THE GUARDIAN* (U.K.), JUNE 2003

When comedians leave the stage and tell somebody "I killed out there!" they usually don't mean that in the literal sense, barring the presence of someone in the audience with a battery-depleted pacemaker.

An exception was a British comic accused of killing in the literal sense following a drunken stunt at the Brighton Sea Life Aquarium. Soused on a bottle of plonk, the man accepted a £1 bet and, in an attempt to gain instant publicity for his comedy show, dove buck-naked into a stingray- and shark-infested aquarium.

The funny-man had put away two bottles of wine before stripping down, jumping over the railing and swimming among the sea creatures. His performance gave a group of schoolchildren, on hand to gaze upon the wonders of the deep, an unexpected glimpse at the pasty flesh of the drunken comedian, clad only in a pair of goggles.

"It is a bit like jumping into a den of lions," said the centre's GM, using an odd analogy to explain the peril of jumping into a tank filled with sharks and potentially paralysis-causing stingrays.

He and other officials were furious at the comedian for his drunken plunge, believing the addition of his unsightly mass into the aquarium upset the delicate balance they had been trying to maintain and wreaked havoc with the sharks' breeding program. Their anger intensified when one of the sharks was found dead three days following the stunt. Suspect number one? The dough-like mass that had descended the aquarium's depths.

An aquarium spokesperson said that the particular variety of shark in question is very susceptible to stress and that the shock of the naked jester's fateful plunge may have killed the creature.

While still considering taking legal action against the man, the aquarium invited him in to participate in feeding time as a goodwill gesture. The comedian, for his part, was less than contrite: "I love fish, especially scampi, and would not willingly harm them."

You're a Mean One, Mr. Inch

REUTERS, JANUARY 2003

"It's not the size of the ship, it's the motion of the ocean" is a pathetic lie commonly voiced by those cursed with less-than-impressive below-the-belt endowment.

The sentiment is clearly hogwash. Most of us know where the preferences of the majority of women would lie on a scale that had tree-squirrel on one end and bull-elephant on the other. Indeed, entire empires have been built out of selling pills, pumps and surgeries to satisfy the average man's desire to add a couple of extra inches to mother nature's allotment. According to the psychiatric sciences, cigar smoking too has something or other to do with small-dicked people.

The most obvious and egregious example of man's preoccupation with his one-eyed gopher is the penis-size competition, in which participants are invited to drop trou. Presumably, the one with third leg nearest the floor wins.

One such competition took place in a village just outside of Manila and ended with deadly consequences. During a drinking party, the host suggested that a penis-size competition would be just the thing to liven up the proceedings.

Remarkably, considering the minor revelation he was about to make, one of his guests complied immediately. Dropping his drawers quicker than a man in the advanced stages of a food-borne illness, he unveiled his Lilliputian marriage tackle to the delight of the assembled, whose raucous hoots and fits of laughter could be heard throughout the village.

The one laughing the loudest was the host, though he was not laughing for long. The exposed man, drunk and angered by the reception his manhood had received, shot and killed the man who had initiated the show-and-tell.

Soldier of Misfortune

MosNews.com (Russia), April 2006

The term *thick-skulled* is usually not meant in the literal sense, which is why if you wanted to place a bet that your head could withstand the force of a brick, Vegas bookmakers would insist on minimum 10–1 odds and a ringside doctor who wasn't busy fixing fights might advise that a hard hat be worn before giving clearance for such a feat.

A former member of the Russian Air Force (considered the military elite, though the behaviour in this case makes a strong case against such a notion) threw a party to celebrate the end of his two-year stint spent serving his country. Not surprisingly, heavy drinking and braggadocio were the order of the day, and at one point the toughness of the party's host was challenged with a dare: a box of vodka if he could break a brick over his head.

Not wanting to leave the challenge in the realm of idle specula-tion, the man hunted around his apartment for a brick, which fortunately for him he did not find. Instead, he improvised and did his best to approximate the dull thud of brick on cranium by smashing empty beer bottles against his head.

One by one the bottles shattered against the man's skull, until he reached the 24th bottle. Then, amidst the applause and encouragement of party-goers, the soldier, who had indeed proved he was a trooper, fell to the floor unconscious.

The party guests, assuming that the man had killed himself and evidently not the greatest of friends, said, "Oh my, look at the time!" or something comparable in Russian, and vamoosed, leaving the poor man's parents to discover him the next morning.

Fortunately, the soldier survived the bashing his head took. He was taken to hospital, where he regained consciousness and then took a page out of his houseguests' book and bolted—presumably to go claim his prize.

Losing Your Head Over a Dare

THE HERALD (U.K.), OCTOBER 1994

A key draw of famed magician Harry Houdini's act in the latter part of his life consisted of calling on audience members to take the stage and punch him in the stomach. He would take the punch without flinching and thus demonstrate the strength of his abs. One day, a student boxer from McGill University in Montreal approached a relaxing, between-shows Houdini and asked him if it was true that he could absorb a punch from anyone in the world. Houdini said yes, and the collegiate boxer proceeded to attack the legendary escape artist. The multiple blows to the gut that the student dished out resulted in a ruptured appendix, of which Houdini eventually died.

While one must assume that Houdini was sober most times he offered to let audience members slug him (a drunk man may find his way into a straitjacket, but the reverse is tricky), this is exactly the kind of dare that one associates with excessively inebriated men. How many of us haven't winded some blowhard by sucker-punching him when he says, "Go on—gimme your best shot"?

The lesson learned from the example set by such idiots and by poor hapless Harry is that it is not wise to call out dares that could somehow result in physical harm to your person.

The lesson would have served one Polish man particularly well. Four friends were in the midst of a heavy session of drinking when one of the four put his hand on a wooden block and dared his friends to chop it off as a demonstration of just how tough a mamma-jamma he was.

None of the three took him up on it, and the drinking continued.

Later, when another member of the party put his head on the block in a similar show of bravado, the man who had previously offered his hand accepted the challenge. Wielding an axe, he separated man and head, and was later arrested for the murder of this indisputably tough guy.

Meet Mr. Yellow-Rat Foxysquirrel Fairydiddle

ANANOVA.COM, SEPTEMBER 2002; MEGASTAR.CO.UK, SEPTEMBER 2002

There are many good reasons for going by a name different from the one you were born with: you're entering a witness protection program, you're running from international law enforcement officials, or you're wanting to distance yourself as far as possible from a book you have written or a movie you have made. Numerous filmmakers, among them Sidney Lumet, Sam Raimi and Dennis Hopper, have, for example, given directing credit in particularly bad films they made to the ubiquitous "Alan Smithee" so as to avoid any stain on their reputations.

An unemployed man from Hertfordshire, England, had a less solid reason for changing his name—he did it in exchange for a pint. Moreover, the rather blandly named Richard James's new moniker is one that would have him held back for extensive questioning and a possible cavity search by any airport customs officer worth the badge: Mr. Yellow-Rat Foxysquirrel Fairydiddle.

In exchange for the pint, Richard let his friends write suggested new names for him on the back of a beer mat. Compiling their contributions, they arrived at the Fairydiddle surname and the ridiculous rest of it and, with the wonder of modern technology, they were able to use a laptop and a credit card to make the whole thing official right away. Herr Fairydiddle informed his bank of his new name and had his credit card switched over as well.

Not long after his buzz wore off, Fairydiddle said he was sick and tired of the jokes surrounding his new moniker and wanted to change it back. Unfortunately for him he was unemployed, and the £38 required to change his name back to Richard was too dear.

IX

The Mourning After: Hangovers—Physical, Emotional and Financial

Ah yes, hangovers: when the glorious lies that you were telling yourself last night come crashing into the truth of today's terrible reality. They are nature's way of reminding you that life is not really as enjoyable as you thought it was when you were doing that waltz with the vacuum cleaner and whistling at your host for another round of margaritas. You wake up with foggy memories of what you were up to on the previous night and a sinking feeling of horror as your mind slowly clears ... and you remember.

Most of the people chronicled in this book probably woke up with a terrible hangover, the pain of which was compounded by having their shame showcased for all to see in the mass media (and by the time they're reading about it again, in this book, the original hangover will have worn off—though they may be driven back to drink).

The Mourning After features those for whom that next day was particularly unpleasant. Even the worst hangover imaginable, when suffered in a bed (and not one in a hospital) is still not as bad as waking up with a pounding head and finding yourself, say, in a sewer, or about to be gobbled up by a trash compactor. From the guy with no criminal record who woke up after a bender realizing he had pulled off a multi-thousand-dollar caper to the guy who had to answer to the media hounding him over a tip for 10 grand that he had left for a waitress on holiday, these are stories with which to comfort yourself the next time you're shouting for Pepto-Bismol and complaining about the weakness of your coffee.

Hangovers, for all their unpleasantness, do teach you something of a lesson, the most pertinent among them being not to drink so much again—or at least to quarter yourself off from others if you do.

In Still Belligerent, we've covered stories of those who learned absolutely nothing from the lesson taught them by their hangovers. On the contrary, waking up the next day with whatever injury was brought on by their own drunken antics, they threw responsibility out the window like so many empties out of a fast-moving pickup truck. While most would think it ridiculous to sue someone else for injuries that occurred when you fell into a snowbank while drunk or scaled an electrical transformer, these people saw their reactions as justified—and in some cases a jury of their (presumably sober) peers agreed with them.

25

Remorseful Drunks (and the People They Owe Apologies To)

A real hangover is nothing to try out family remedies on.
The only cure for a real hangover is death.

—ROBERT BENCHLEY

The Outspoken Spokesman

THE SCOTSMAN, JANUARY 2000; SUNDAY MAIL (AUSTRALIA), JUNE 2000

One of the less pleasant aspects of a night of pie-eyed gallivanting is the prospect of having to atone the following day for one's actions. Apologies of this sort usually entail having to tell your significant other that you "didn't mean anything" when you drunkenly asked if her best friend's marriage was a liberal one.

Imagine, though, having to apologize to every one of the people who had to bear your drunken presence over the course of an evening—the "little people," as it were, who ferried you around in taxis or served you in fast-food stalls while you were quipping faster than an amphetamine-charged Truman Capote.

Most of us would just chock up the unpleasantness borne by these people as having to do with their karmic debt. But a 51-year-old accountant from Wales felt so bad about his actions on an evening that began at a hotel and ended 10 wildly drunk hours later that he took out a public notice in the *Western Mail* to apologize to all those he had offended.

With the specifics adjusted, the apology could serve as a template for other drunks looking to make amends. Written in the third person, but bearing his name at the end, it read: "He would like to say sorry to the entire staff of the Cardiff Hilton Hotel, several city centre landlords, the residents of Prospect Drive, a man called Toni at a fish bar, two passing police constables and the council cleansing department.

"Most particularly he offers this public apology to those whose love and affection he values more than life itself. All those people, and doubtless many more, were at some time during a long night, castigated, vilified, embarrassed or, worse, bored, for which he most humbly and respectfully apologizes."

While "a man called Toni at a fish bar" has never publicly acknowledged the apology, the Association of Chartered Accountants, of which the letter writer had been a spokesman, did. They rewarded his public blame-taking by forcing his resignation.

The association said in a statement that the spokesman could just as easily have gone to the people he met on New Year's Eve and apologized to them individually, rather than taking out the newspaper ad, which did not "reflect well on the profession of accountancy."

The International Language of Hangovers

Hangovers and travelling seem to go hand in hand, so here, for the globetrotting among you, are a few terms for hangovers from different countries, each capturing a particular nuance of that next-day suffering:

- **Portugal:** *ressaca* (*resaca* in Spain), meaning "undertow," in reference to the fact that your stomach feels as if it is navigating choppy waters
- **Slovakia:** *mat opicu,* which literally, and perhaps as a testament to the boisterous nights out in this country, translates as "to have a monkey"
- **France:** many terms, though the most common is *la gueule de bois,* meaning "wooden mouth," because of the sandpapery dry-mouth feeling of a hangover
- **Denmark:** *tømmermænd,* which means "timber men," or carpenters, likening the pounding headache of an unforgiving hangover to construction work taking place inside your head
- **Germany:** *der Katzenjammer, or der Kater,* which means "the wailing of the cats," nicely capturing the overall soul-killing pain of a hangover

(*EasyJet Magazine,* October 2005)

Getting Trashed

WKRC (U.S.), September 2005

For the ill-fed, or simply the plain cheap, Dumpster diving is a not entirely socially accepted means of making one man's trash another's breakfast. Dangers do exist at the "compost cafeteria," such as when the mall fast-food joint dumps out its barrel of daily hot grease (such stories circulate) or when you contract an unlucky bout of salmonella from an ill-begotten burger.

For the garbage gourmand, however, there exists a more forbidding danger: Mondays and Thursdays, or alternating days depending on the pickup schedule in your area.

A Cincinnati man capped off a night of partying and boozing by climbing into a downtown Dumpster and falling asleep. The next morning, having forgotten entirely that immutable law that says Dumpsters must periodically be dumped, he was nearly dispatched to that great blue box in the sky by the unforgiving teeth of a trash truck.

On pickup day, the man we'll call "Bin-boy" was sleeping soundly as the garbage truck driver pulled in for his scheduled run. He had what was undoubtedly a rude (and odiferous) awakening a few moments later. A local woman, hearing the plaintive screams that one could imagine a person in such a situation would be driven to release, flagged down the driver, telling him that there was someone in the Dumpster.

Looking back on Bin-boy's brush with horrifying death, an eyewitness responded with a hearty guffaw, saying that "it was kind of comical to see somebody actually come out of a Dumpster truck."

It Could Happen to You ... or Not

CHICAGO SUN-TIMES, JUNE 2000; *LONDON TELEGRAPH*, JUNE 2000

In the 1994 feel-good movie *It Could Happen to You*, Nicholas Cage played a New York City cop who, in lieu of a tip, promises to give his waitress half of his winnings should he hit the jackpot in the state lottery, and later, when he does win, delivers on the promise. That movie was based on a true story—in 1984 a waitress in Yonkers, New York, met such good fortune.

Although the premise is similar, a generous tipper giving a hard-working waitress a tip that is the stuff of dreams, the man who left the fat tip in this story has more in common with Cage's character in his Oscar-winning turn as a drunkard in *Leaving Las Vegas.*

At 3:30 A.M. one day, a 35-year-old Briton walked into the Leg Room, which despite the obvious connotations of its name is actually a trendy Chicago nightspot, with two other men and ordered a Long Island Iced Tea from a 23-year-old waitress.

As many bar frequenters before him have done and many will continue to do, the customer began to chat up the young woman in his best "guy trying to pick up a waitress near closing time" fashion. He told her that he was a visiting "doctor" (in actual fact he worked in software) and asked her about her dreams and aspirations. She told him that one day she would like to go to graduate school.

The waitress said that the customer then told her to go chase her dreams and become a doctor just like him. To help her on her way, he penned a $10,000 tip onto the credit-card payment slip for his $9 bill.

The manager at the Leg Room was alerted to the generosity of the customer and later said that he took measures to ensure that the offer was genuine, even photocopying the man's passport and getting him to sign a piece of paper saying he gave the tip in good faith.

The tip cleared that night but was later rejected, as it exceeded the "doctor's" maximum limit on his Visa card.

The Brit, upon returning home, was hounded by the media and asked why he reneged on the princely sum. He claimed that someone had "clearly taken advantage of my drunken state in that bar," and that he had no memory of the night or of leaving the tip and the entire episode had been a nightmare. He just wanted the whole thing to be forgotten.

Unlike most in this book, this story does indeed have a happy Hollywood ending. The bar's owner, overjoyed at all the free press his bar received as a result of the incident, cut the waitress a cheque for the missing 10 G's.

Waking Up on the Wrong Side of the Drainage System

The Australian, January 1996

Greeting the morning in a strange place is old hat to the dedicated drunkard, and guessing where you might do so is half the fun. There are some places—unlike, say, a stranger's bed—where you wouldn't want to end up: a mental hospital, a prison, backstage at a death metal concert, or the nasty spot where the celebrating gent in this story did. The sewer.

The man, 51, was returning from an end-of-year office party in Seoul, South Korea, on December 28 and was, as one would be after any office party worth its salt, quite drunk. Oblivious to where he was going as he sauntered down the road, the partier slipped through an open manhole over a sewer and plunged 18 feet. After the fall, he fell into a deep sleep.

Waking up the next morning amid the reeking sewage, he said, he then set out in search of an exit.

The man made do with what little supplies he could scrounge together in his new subterranean home, staving off dehydration, he said, by drinking from a puddle of clean water that he had come across, sleeping on a foam mat that some thoughtful polluter had dumped down there for him, and using a wooden stick to guide himself through the dark tunnel. He also covered his head and legs with plastic bags to help ward off the chill, keeping a watchful eye out for those full-grown pet alligators that, if urban legends have taught us anything, have been flushed by their petrified owners.

After eight days spent poking around a cold, dark, filthy sewer looking for a way out, his mournful cries were finally heard by a woman in a nearby apartment. While he claimed he had walked several miles in search of an exit, rescue workers say they found the sewered celebrant only about 150 feet from the spot where he took the plunge.

Act Vile, You're on Candid Camera!

The Advertiser (Australia), May 1997

There are many reasons why you don't want a video camera anywhere near you when you're drunk. Telling your hosts with a glassy sneer on your face how much affection you have for them may seem like a beautiful moment while it's taking place, but put that emotional outpouring on video for posterity and you will have something to shame you for years to come—or at least until the technology employed in its recording becomes obsolete.

If you think there is even the slightest possibility that you might commit an actionable offence, you are well advised to make sure that nobody is taping your actions. Disregard this advice and you run the risk of waking up one day like an Australian man did, turning on the television and watching home video footage of a drunken yob out on a tear, and coming to the slow, horrible realization that you are said yob.

The man in question started off at a stag party held for a friend, and later, quite inebriated, boarded a train with a group at Mount Druitt Station. Not wanting to miss one precious moment of the performance being put on by the blasted man, his buddy took out a video camera.

The drunkard's first act captured on film was his verbal harassment of a female passenger. When satisfied that he had provided this stranger with adequate abuse, he then turned his attention to the train's furnishings, specifically a bench seat. His other friends held open the train doors and gave him a three-count, after which he made the thumbs-up sign for the camera and sent the train seat hurtling out into the night.

The man later claimed to have no recollection of his escapades on the train, though he owned up to what he had done after seeing the tape played on the program *A Current Affair* and realizing, in what must have been a terrible day-after moment, that he was the drunken idiot on display.

In court, the presiding magistrate called the actions depicted on the video "lunacy" and "drunken loutish behaviour," and sentenced him to 200 hours of community service.

Nacho Nacho Man ... I Don't Wanna Be This Nacho Man

DAILY TIMES (U.S.), JULY 2004

The morning after your birthday blowout, your sense that you are driving the pace car in the Grand Prix of Life may be further cemented as you recall the events of the previous night. While you are indeed one year older, you are most certainly not any the wiser, you realize as you recall those slobber-filled non-sequiturs, put-on Irish brogues and that difference of opinion with the Cowboys fan. In most cases, you can put such terrible events behind you with a combination of pills, colonic irrigation and a kind circle of friends; however, one Tennessee man was forced to relive his agonizing birthday memories in print, and in court—and yet again if he ever picks up this book.

Only the most hardened detective could've stomached the birthday boy's shenanigans, worthy of the immediate deployment of yellow police tape.

The 23-year-old, in a vodka-induced miasma, left his Jeep parked outside of a community swimming pool with the intention of scaling the 8-foot fence surrounding it and raiding the snack bar. He did so, lifting a box of snacks, and also left a calling card by losing bowel control in a garbage can—all of this while in the nude, no less. If that wasn't enough (and in going over the details of this case, we can safely say it was), the man also ended up with processed nacho cheese smeared all over his hair, face and shoulders. He was apprehended by police while running naked back to his Jeep and clutching the box of snacks—the product of an unnamed snack-food company for which any publicity is not necessarily good publicity.

Don't Talk to Strangers

THE ADVERTISER (AUSTRALIA), SEPTEMBER 1997

There is probably no more common a setting for the planning of idiotic criminal escapades than your corner bar. Get to drinking in one low-rent establishment for long enough and you're bound to at least overhear some indiscreet patron blab about how easy street would be around the next corner if only he, or she, could carry off the perfect score.

While most people would wisely choose to focus on their beer nuts and the *Wheel of Fortune* playing on the television, some poor saps like the one in this story actually carry out such ill-conceived and alcohol-fuelled plans.

The man had been going through family and financial problems and had decided to take his sorrows out for a drowning. As his mind clouded over with drink, he struck up a sob-story barroom conversation with another guy, who identified himself only as "Rob."

Hearing the man's tale of woe, Rob offered him a sure-fire way out of his financial constraints, saying that he had the keys to a company in the area and that all our drunken friend had to do was help out and he would land himself a cool couple of grand.

The man agreed to take part in Rob's scheme and, though he said later that he remembers little of what happened next, the two then went on to raid the company, stealing a car and filling it with items, including computer equipment. The total value of the haul was $93,000.

The next morning, the man awoke at his own workplace with Rob nowhere in sight and most of the stolen loot in the car parked outside.

Made more than a little anxious by this discovery, he dropped off the car in another part of town, hoping that someone would find it and return the vehicle to its owners, and when that didn't happen after a week had elapsed, he hid the loot in a friend's shed.

Police eventually found the man, using fingerprints left at the crime scene, and arrested him. Most of the loot was returned. The judge, hearing his tale of drunken influence, showed clemency and did not give him any jail time.

The Martini Marriage

SUNDAY TELEGRAPH (U.K.), NOVEMBER 2001; BBC, NOVEMBER 2001

Travellers come to Las Vegas with certain preconceived notions of what the city offers: the debauched gambling, the headliners, the numerous stoolies lying in unmarked graves in the hot surrounding desert—and right up there with all of these is the Vegas quickie wedding. Hundreds of thousands of couples, with perhaps not the greatest reverence for the institution of marriage, have been hitched in Sin City ever since Bugsy Siegel first laid eyes on it and thought what a great place it would be for the mob.

A Bristol University student stopped in Vegas while backpacking around the United States with a friend and decided, once he was there, to partake of the full Vegas experience. Since he had already gambled and gotten rip-roaring drunk, the only item left on his tour itinerary was getting married amid all that neon and filthy lucre. Luckily, a fellow traveller, a 26-year-old optician from Australia, was happy to fill the role of temporary bride for a lark before they went their own ways the next day.

He suggested that they take their stumble down the aisle at the Candlelight Wedding Chapel, one of Vegas's best-known quickie nuptial joints—one that had previously witnessed the rushed "I do's" of Whoopi Goldberg, Bette Midler, Michael Caine and Noel Gallagher (to be clear, these people did not marry one another).

For the ceremony at the Candlelight the groom was decked out in his very best, just-pulled-from-backpack scruffy shirt and trousers, as well as a copper ring he had borrowed to place on the finger of his betrothed. Following the wedding, a small reception was held during which guests feasted, as well as they could, on Twinkies (sponge cakes with an "oh so creamy" centre) washed back with champagne. The bride is said to have passed out during the wedding breakfast the following morning.

Back in England after his journey, the collegian couldn't wait to tell his entertaining Vegas tale to everyone, including his long-term girlfriend. She listened with good humour to the saga until he arrived at the part where he had married another woman. She turned cold and dumped him before he could plead his case.

His parents had a very mixed reaction: his dad laughed, his mother wept.

The man's bride was still travelling when the story broke. As for the groom, the entire episode was one he would live to regret, both because of the shock it delivered to his girlfriend and mother and also the recurring headaches that resulted—when he had to register as a married man at his college dorm, for example.

He later sought to have the marriage annulled on the grounds that the newlyweds were too drunk on their wedding night to consummate their union back at the youth hostel.

World's Worst Instant Coffee

THE DAILY MAIL (U.K.), NOVEMBER 2004

Hangovers can bring about horrible physical sensations for an otherwise healthy person who typically avoids sources of sickness such as restaurant buffets and who's had all the proper inoculations. The next morning your overall constitution seems to have taken an unworldly walloping while you slept, and aches start festering in places that you had previously been unaware supported the workings of muscles. It's not unusual for you to suffer nausea, or worse, and for your gastrointestinal workings to enter a state of deep uncertainty.

What weapon does mankind have against this onslaught of unpleasantness brought on by the joys of drinking? There isn't one. The best solution that has turned up so far is drinking coffee; though it won't cure what ails you, the caffeine shock will at least distract you.

Coffee is what a group of friends staying at a country cottage in the Czech Republic were after when they woke up hungover from the merriment of the night before. In their befuddled state, they did a quick search of the cabin and found a tin containing a grainy substance—instant coffee, they must have assumed, that had been hanging out in the old cottage for some time.

They spooned it out into cups, poured hot water over it and drank it down, thinking that it did taste a bit odd, but chalking that up to its age.

It should be mentioned at this point that the tin of coffee the friends found was taken down from the cabin's mantelpiece.

When the owner of the cabin realized what they had done, he exclaimed: "You idiots, you've drunk my grandfather's remains!"

One of the friends said the group sobered up immediately—the shock clearly having worked even better than caffeine would have.

The grandson took the incident in stride and said that his grandfather, a man with a good sense of humour, was probably looking down at the lot of them and laughing.

26

Still Belligerent: Drunks Who Sue

Never stir up litigation. A worse man can scarcely be found than one who does this.

—ABRAHAM LINCOLN

The $850,000 Snow Dive

NORTHJERSEY MEDIA GROUP, OCTOBER 2004;
KANSAS CITY STAR, NOVEMBER 2004

Next time you go out for a walk while fully tanked in the middle of the winter and end up face down in a snowbank, before hastily judging yourself a hopeless, clumsy moron, take a moment to consider the following story.

A New Jersey guy was celebrating New Year's 2001 by partying it up with a group of his friends at a hotel on the outskirts of town. Once the countdown was over and things had begun to wind down, the reveller decided he needed something to eat and some cigarettes, and set out in search of both along the rural road wearing a leather coat, a sweater and jeans.

Realizing that all the restaurants were closed for the night, the partier attempted to head back to the hotel, but in his inebriated condition this was not to be. He ended up wandering into the parking lot of an area restaurant and, possibly seeing the great white light before him, walked directly into a snowbank and did a swan dive into it.

Nearly an hour went by before someone spotted him and, realizing that he was not attempting to make a snow angel, phoned police. A cruiser arrived in the area, but somehow the cops missed seeing the man splayed out in the Jersey snow like something from a popular HBO mobster program.

Hours went by before a customer at the restaurant, in for his morning coffee, again spotted the man in the snow and phoned police. This time cops rushed to the scene, found him and pulled him out of the snowbank, took precautions against hypothermia, which the high level of alcohol in his blood would have hastened, and set about reviving him before taking him to hospital. He was later treated for frostbite to his hand.

That hand, left disfigured as a result of the incident, became the basis for a lawsuit the man filed against the local and county police. His claim was that police did not do enough to track him down after the first emergency call, and that as a result they should cough up some cash.

Incredibly, the man received an $850,000 payday for his drunken snooze in the snow.

The Rights of Public Drunks

A Boston man who was arrested at a New Year's Eve party launched a lawsuit to challenge a Massachusetts law that allows cops to lock up drunks against their will for their own protection. (MSNBC.com, July 8, 2005)

DISHONOURABLE MENTION
Chair of the Drinking Committee

Bar stools come in all shapes and styles: retro, swivel, wooden, wrought iron, or, for those who can't resist living dangerously—backless swivel. Given that they top out at a height of roughly 3 feet, a tumble from such a precipice would result in serious injury—especially if one were situated at the edge of a cliff, or more realistically, beside a long flight of stairs.

Trying the mettle and fortitude of the judiciary, a barfly asked the Maryland Court of Special Appeals to allow him to go ahead with a lawsuit against a tavern in Baltimore for damages incurred when, after a day squandered in a marathon drinking extravaganza, he keeled over and fell off his bar stool.

But try as he might, he could not convince the court that as a drunk, and injured, customer he had a "civil cause of action against the bar or tavern owner."

He lost his appeal, and there is no word if he has climbed back up on a bar-side squatter since his fall from grace. (*Washington Post*, December 1982)

All We Hear Is Radio Ga-Ga

THE INDEPENDENT (U.K.), MARCH 2003; *BLOOMBERG NEWS,* JUNE 2003; *THE SCOTSMAN,* JUNE 2003

No morning radio show is complete without slide whistles, alien-landing sound effects, or a crazy cuckoo hooting away. With these tools as their stock in trade, it's no surprise that on occasion these pre-dawn fart-joke jocks are driven straight to the nearest and fullest bottle.

An English radio presenter and his trusty sidekick were taking part in a promotional stunt that would have had them staying on the air for 14 hours straight leading up to a big international football match. The DJ figured the stunt would be great publicity for the station and, presumably in order to strengthen his resolve and that of his sidekick, he decided that a few pre–sun-up pints were in order.

The slurring of words, cussing and complete dearth of wit that was being broadcast didn't immediately clue in their employer to the fact that something was amiss, this likely being business as usual for the moribund duo. Eventually, however, the station did get wind of the pair's antics and refused to allow them to continue the broadcast. The DJs were forced to sign off, which they did in style, closing with a drunken though succinct on-air "Sod them!"

The presenter lost his job over the incident and as a result launched a lawsuit claiming that the radio station had withheld millions of British pounds in share options after terminating his contract. For his failure to show up for a series of broadcasts, he blamed a drinking spree that he went on because he was "put under so much pressure by management at the station."

The radio station, meanwhile, claimed that the man's antics, specifically a certain three-day bender, were damaging to its reputation. The judge in this case labelled the man a binge drinker, saying: "He told me with pride that more often than not he presented the show with a hangover."

This defence, not exactly the product of a brilliant legal mind, sealed the man's fate: the judge determined that he had clearly broken the terms of his contract and found in favour of the station.

Putting the Ale in Sales

FOX NEWS, JANUARY 2006; CNN, JANUARY 2006;
QUEENSLAND NEWS PRESS, OCTOBER 1998

The plant manager at a Michigan Ford production facility recently announced that the parking lot could be used only by employees driving vehicles built by Ford or one of its subsidiaries. To some, punishing employees for how they spend their own money is the epitome of gall, while to others it makes good business sense to enforce brand loyalty at home at all costs.

An Australian sales rep for a major international brewer was fired for going on a 10-hour drinking binge that involved downing several beers, wine and assorted spirits at a sales conference. Possibly he would not have found himself in such a pickled pickle had he taken a page out of Ford's manual and stuck to drinking pints of his employer's hooch. But we're just speculating.

The man quaffed whatever he could—pints of his product along with other sundry drinks—and later was found sauntering around the resort in the buff, abusing colleagues and staff. He also was said to have gotten into a squabble with the resident DJ, who, being a resort disc jockey, may or may not—reports do not indicate—have been playing the execrable steel-drum-laden Beach Boys tune "Kokomo."

The court was told that the rep and a colleague—the latter had the good sense to resign over his own "abominable behaviour"— went skinny-dipping in the resort pool in front of other company employees and were naked when confronted by a resort guest woken by their antics.

The brewer dispatched the sales rep for his nude cavorting at the resort. A two-and-a-half-year legal battle ensued, centring on his argument that his drunken behaviour was the result of the company plying him with "copious amounts" of alcohol during the four-day conference.

Once the litigation was over, the Industrial Court of Australia determined the brewer's dismissal unlawful, and ordered his higher-ups to fork over $100,000 and return the man to his post. Before he could hoist a few celebratory pints, the Federal Court overturned that decision.

If at first you don't succeed (in convincing others that your abhorrent, embarrassing behaviour is actually their fault), try, try again, and so he did, launching and eventually winning an action with the Full Court of Appeals that questioned the Federal Court's decision. In the end, he got back his well-salaried, perk-laden job, free drinks and all.

A Shocker of a Lawsuit

REUTERS, MARCH 2000; *TAMPA TRIBUNE*, MARCH 2000

Of all the fraudulent ways there are to avoid a life of hard, honest work, winning a frivolous lawsuit and living off the spoils is undoubtedly right up there. Run, don't walk, when you spot a spill on the floor of your local Shop and Bag It, and once the initial pain of dislocating your shoulder subsides, you will be sitting pretty.

A caution, though. If you decide to chase lawsuit money you must first consider whether any jury member with the sense to find his or her own seat in the jury box will give you the time of day if the events leading up to your injury comprised your getting pie-eyed drunk and ignoring every safety measure possible to protect you from yourself.

A Florida man thought just such an argument would fly when he filed a lawsuit relating to the injuries he sustained after capping off a drunken night on the town. The sozzled son of the Sunshine State found his way into an electric-company substation, despite its being fenced off and locked, and scaled the transformer. His reward? He was zapped with 13,000 volts—more than twice the voltage used on those who get to visit Ol' Sparky after being on Death Row—and thrown 40 feet.

The man suffered burns, and eventually filed a claim in court based on that as well as on emotional suffering against the electric company for not doing a better job of keeping him from electrocuting himself. He also filed suit against the places he claimed sold him the booze that inspired him to undertake the feat, which included two sports bars, a roadhouse restaurant, a convenience store, a grocery story and a gas station.

His lawsuit said that since he is "unable to control his urge to drink," the bars and stores were negligent in serving or selling him alcohol.

One of the bar-owners upon whose shoulders this drunken Floridian placed the blame for his injuries called the lawsuit frivolous and denied that the man had even made an appearance at his establishment on the stated night. According to the bartender, the plaintiff had earlier been banned from the bar for writing on the bathroom walls.

A spokesman for the utility said that it was company policy not to comment on the man's lawsuit, though she told reporters that "It's hard not to."

Wrong Man at the Switch

The first known incident of an unsuccessful execution in the United States occurred in 1946 in Louisiana when the state tried to electrocute Willie Francis but failed because the chair had been improperly hooked up by an intoxicated trustee. (Wikipedia.com)

No Longer a Spotless Record

DAILY NEWS (U.S.), MARCH 1996; *NEW ZEALAND LISTENER,* MAY–JUNE 2005

If extreme chef Anthony Bourdain is correct (and there's no reason to doubt him, because he's written a book), his business attracts dysfunctional types—criminals, reprobates, alcoholics and other social misfits. Yet the famous TV chef opposes mandatory drug testing for kitchen staff because he insists, basically, that a kitchen is a meritocracy and those who can, do pull themselves up by their apron strings.

The same cannot be said for a New York City dishwasher, who, perhaps sensing his immediate career path wasn't going to include chicken artichoke linguine in béchamel sauce but plenty of detergent-related dermatitis, launched a lawsuit against the NYC Transit Authority for allowing him to stumble drunk into the path of an oncoming subway train.

The man won a lawsuit awarding him $9.3 million in damages for losing a limb in the first trial (well, he didn't lose it in the trial— he lost it in the train mishap), a number that one legal analyst at the time said would have made sense if the man was, say, a millionaire athlete who reasonably could have been expected to earn such a sum within the next 300 years.

A subsequent court struck down that finding, and later an appeals court tossed out another verdict, like so many rotten bags of Swiss chard, that would have awarded the man $3 million in damages.

In both cases, the courts decided that the transit authority was not responsible for the accident at the Bronx station, despite claims by lawyers that the tracks were not lit well enough to allow the conductor to see their intoxicated client before the train hit him.

Pork-Chop Challenge

Daily Telegraph (Australia), June 2002

As a youngster you receive a cuff on the back of the head for playing with your food. You're told it is both rude and gluttonous to behave that way in a world where so many have so little to eat. As we get older and are out of our mothers' slapping reach, we no longer have to follow these rules and can indeed snort chickpeas up our noses, mime giving birth to a head of lettuce or, as one Australian man did, use pork chops in a unique manner.

While out enjoying a night of heavy drinking with friends, the Aussie was inspired to dump his pork chops on the floor, tie them to his feet and parade around the restaurant, even improvising pork-chop skateboarding. He did this to the delight of his friends, who cheered him on. In fact, when his performance was over, the other patrons in the restaurant picked up some of the meat and fat he had left behind and started a food fight.

Amid all of this pork-chop pandemonium, the entertainer's friend, who reportedly had been as enthusiastic as the others up until that point, slipped on the grease, fell and broke his arm. No longer laughing, he decided to sue his long-time friend for causing the injury.

Fortunately, the judge who heard the case did not find fault in the pork-chop performer's actions, but rather thought that the inn in which the incident took place should have done a better job of supervising its customers and keeping the floors clean. He ordered the inn to fork over $61,515 to the plaintiff for his injury. But he ordered the plaintiff in turn to look after the defendant's legal costs.

The restaurant performer said later that the lawsuit had put a strain on the pair's friendship, but admitted that the incident had taught him a valuable lesson—he said he would not employ pork in such a manner again, preferring as he did an open-toed sandal.

Acknowledgments

The authors would like to thank our agent Anastasia Silva and Helen Reeves at Penguin Group (Canada) for their long-term support the entire way, as well as our friends and family members, too numerous to name here but they know who they are, particularly Linda Boivin and Martin Bryan and Inge and Olando Lombardo, and for their help and encouragement Laura Thrasher, Pamela Lindsay, Matthew Hindman, Tamas Pal, Pamela Cottrell, Chanyanuch Chaisorn and Michelle Tapp. And thanks also to the bars that poured out much inspiration for us, in particular our regular haunts of Hurricanes Roadhouse and the Cadillac Lounge in Toronto and the Merchant Ale House in St. Catharines.